Dangerous Flashpoints in East Asia: The Military Build-up

SAGHIR IQBAL

ISBN:1974062309
ISBN-13: 978-1974062300

DEDICATION

I dedicate this book to all those who gave me encouragement, support and guidance. Foremost, to my father (late) Raja Mohammed Iqbal and to Professor Syed Peerzada Mahmud Shah Bookhari, from whom I have learnt so much. In addition to my wife Neghat Khan, who was patient and extremely helpful in my trying times. And finally I dedicate this to my three colleagues – Mohammed Rafiq, Tahir Bashir and Fiaz Nabi.

CONTENTS

ACKNOWLEDGMENTS

I am very grateful to a host of people for their various contributions towards this book. I am particularly very grateful to Professor Syed Peerzada Mahmud Shah Bookhari who deserves much commendation for his constant encouragement and support throughout the hard times of the programme.

Dangerous Flashpoints in East Asia: The Military Build-up

Image/pixabay.com/soldiers training

Abstract

Major changes in East Asia have placed the region near the top of the World's strategic agenda. East Asia has until recently experienced the fastest regional economic growth rate in the world for many years. Economic co-operation has been flourishing and economic interests have become the major reason in reshaping East Asian international relations. However, there have also been changes in the security environment, due to many factors, such as the reduction of US forces in East Asia, the disintegration of the Soviet Union (the decline of the Soviet Union's presence in the region had led to renewed attention to traditional and potential rivalries among the major East Asian powers), and the concern of China's hegemonistic ambitions. The economic boom and technological progress in East Asia has made the area a market for the most advanced military systems. The countries in this region are changing their present land-oriented armed forces into modern military institutions composing of well-equipped air and naval units which would enable them to deploy military force at sea as well as to far away places, thereby providing them with a capacity for 'power projection'

Some of the key powers in this region are using antiaccess/area-denial (A2/AD) capabilities to hold their rivals at bay whilst enforcing expansive territorial claims. This book focuses briefly on the disputes, the arms build-up and conflict prevention.. It maintains that the rapid economic growth in East Asia will reduce the risk of war but this alone is not adequate to preserve regional peace and security, especially when the rapid advance in economic growth has also resulted in a massive arms build-up. Therefore additional factors need to be taken into account such as confidence building measures to achieve peace in the region.

Images/pixabay.com/Soldiers on parade and F-15 Eagle combat aircraft

Abbreviation

AAR - Air to air refuelling

A2/AD – Anti-access/Area-denial

AIFV – Armoured Infantry Fighting Vehicle

APC – Armoured Personnel Carrier

ALCM/GLCM – Air Launched Cruise Missile/ Ground Launched Cruise Missile

APEC - Asia-Pacific Economic Cooperation (APEC)

ARF - ASEAN Regional Forum (ARF)

ASEAN - Association of Southeast Asian Nations

AWACS – Airborne Warning and Control System

GDP - Gross Domestic Product

EEZ - Exclusive Economic Zone

ICBM - Intercontinental Ballistic Missile

LT TK – Light Tank

MBT – Main Battle Tank

PGM - Precision guided munitions (Smart weapons)

SAM – Surface to Air Missile

UAV – Unmanned Aerial Vehicle

UCAV – Unmanned Combat Aerial Vehicle

UN – United Nations

UNCLOS - United Nations Convention on the Law of the Sea

WMD – Weapons of Mass Destruction

Images/pixabay.com/Silhouette of an F-16 Falcon combat aircraft

Chapter 1: East Asia's Conflicts of Interests

Image/pixabay.com/helicopters parked during a storm

The rapid economic growth in East Asia has had a profound effect on the region. The income generated in this region has doubled in the last decade, and appears set to double once again.[1] The economic growth has improved the standard of life in nearly all East Asian nations and has industrialized a substantial part of the countries, but it has also led to an increase in defence expenditure. The economic phenomenon in the region has allowed most governments to fund ambitious arms purchases without increased burdens upon their economies.[2]

The explanations for this increase in defence expenditure are due to the many maritime and territorial disputes in the area and that these tensions have created suspicion and misunderstandings and in some instances have provoked armed clashes (such as those in the South China Sea). Hence, there remains much breeding grounds for regional conflict. Many of the disputes are over competing sovereignty claims, challenges to government legitimacy, and territorial disputes.[3]

---

4. Chalmers, Greens & Zhiqiong, op cit:15

5. Brown, op cit:79

6. Brown, op cit:85

Furthermore, as the countries in this region industrialize and become more dependent on global trade, they also tend to see a need to protect the free flow of worldwide trade as well as offshore resources such as ocean fisheries and undersea oil supplies. These strategic interests have led to the enlargement and modernization of air and naval units. Thus, the increase wealth in the region has contributed to an increase in the defence budget, this was itself motivated by the persistence of regional disputes. In addition, the cases of right-wing nationalism, jingoism, chauvinism have begun to show in the region. This atmosphere can make it very difficult for peaceful resolution of potential conflicts in the region.

Overall the region is plagued with many problems ranging from territorial disputes to the proliferation of weapons of mass destruction, this could cause instability in the area unless confidence-building measures are introduced.

1.   Altogether in East Asia there are two distinct zones of tension that have resulted in sophisticated arms being procured. We shall mention some of these disputes very briefly.

(1) - **<u>North-East Asia-</u>** This part of the area mainly focuses on North and South Korea, Japan, Russia, China and Taiwan. Primarily North Korea remains a source of unpredictability and a likely danger for the region. Its extreme emphasis on military enlargement at the cost of essential economic, political and social development poses a threat to its neighbours and regional stability. Even with a badly shrinking economy and years of insufficient harvests, North Korea has given priority to its military stance.[4]

Many territorial disputes that have occasionally led to regional conflict in East Asia could lead to further instability in this region. The island disputes are primarily over small, sparsely populated land that are normally isolated from the countries' mainland. The importance to the areas is due to the abundant natural resources and strategic interests that lie in this part of the world.[5] The following Islands are in dispute:

The Diaoyu (Senkaku) Islands – China, Taiwan and Japan

The Diaoyu/Senkaku Islands have been claimed by China, Taiwan and Japan. The Islands were previously controlled by Taiwan as part of China but during the Sino-Japanese war were captured by Japan. After World War 2, Taiwan was handed back to China but no status was defined for the Islands. In 1971 the USA and Japan signed a treaty in which Okinawa and the Islands were given to Japanese control. China had protested against this decision and had challenged the agreement.

The Islands are normally barren but the surrounding waters contain oil and natural gas and also serve as fishing grounds. This claim of natural resources has reinvigorated the dispute in this area.[6]

---

7.   Chalmers, Greene & Zhiqiong, op cit:17

[5] Ben Dolven, Mark Manyin, Shirley Kan, Maritime Territorial Disputes in East Asia: Issues for Congress, CRS Report, 2014

[6] http://www.newstown.co.kr/news/articleView.html?idxno=128309

Dokdo (Takeshima) Islands – Korea and Japan;

A dispute over the Island chain in the Sea of Japan has resulted in tension between South Korea and Japan. South Korea claims the Islands as the Dokdo Islands and Japan as the Takeshima Islands. Japan argues that the Island had been claimed prior to annexation of South Korea during its colonisation era. South Korea states that the Island became its territory when it declared independence in 1945. The islands are patrolled by South Korean police and tension had increased in January 2011 when the captain of a South Korean Fishing vessel that was operating in the disputed area had been arrested by Japan.[7]

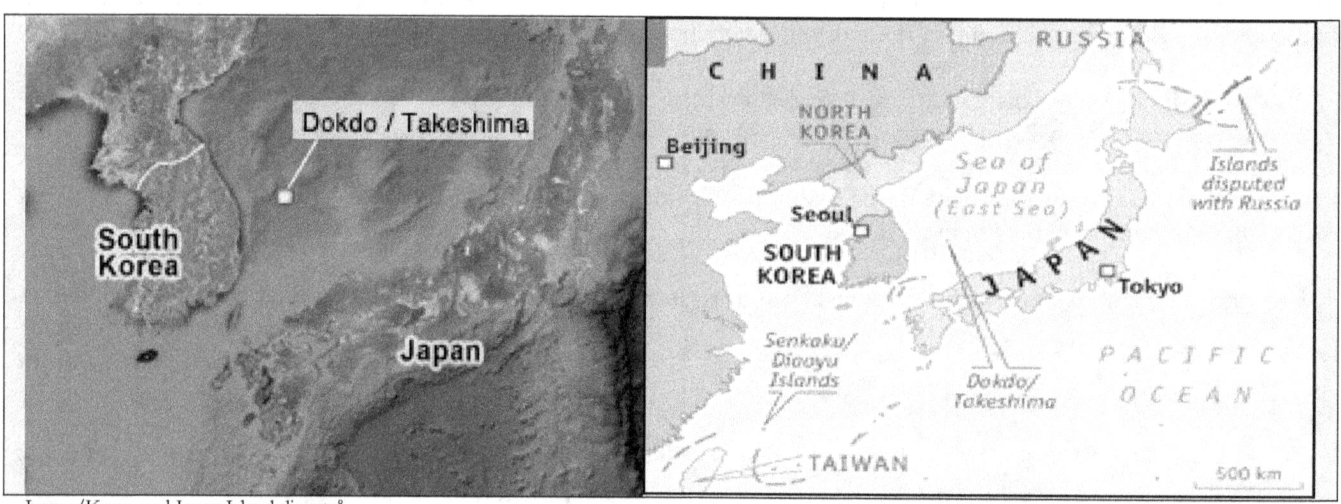

Image/Korea and Japan Island dispute[8]

Image/Kuril Islands dispute[9]

The Kuril Islands – claimed by Japan and Russia.

The Southern Kuril Islands were occupied by the Soviet Union in 1945. The Russian government has argued that these Islands were granted to them during the Post-World War 2 agreements (Yalta and Potsdam agreement). However Japan states that they had been illegally seized by the Soviet Union and had always been an integral part of Japan.

A formal peace treaty was never signed after World War 2 due to the Kuril Islands dispute. A diplomatic rift reopened in 2010 when the Russian President Dmitry Medvedev's visited the disputed Islands. The United States of America has been a staunch long-time supporter of Japan's claims to the disputed territory.

---

[7] Leigh Montgomery (2011), East Asia's Top 5 Island disputes, Online - https://www.csmonitor.com/World/Asia-Pacific/2011/0803/East-Asia-s-top-5-island-disputes/Takeshima-Dokdo-islands-claimed-by-Japan-and-South-Korea
[8] https://www.voanews.com/a/japan-protests-south-korean-media-tour-to-disputed-isle/1520848.html
http://asw.newpacificinstitute.org/?p=10440

[9] https://www.pinterest.co.uk/pin/383720830722127190/

Yeonpyeong Island – claimed by North Korea and South Korea

Tensions over the island have occasionally escalated and fatal fire was traded twice in 2010 – once when North Korea unexpectedly shelled the island and another time when it torpedoed a South Korean naval vessel. Military drills by both countries in the area have raised international concerns.

A dispute over the Islands of Yeonpyeong by North and South Korea had escalated into a fire fight in 2010. The Island had been shelled by North Korean artillery and a South Korean Naval ship was also torpedoed. These Islands have been in dispute when the UN and North Korea failed to agree on a boundary. The Islands lie very close to the North Korean Mainland (approximately 8 miles distance) but is claimed by South Korea as part of the North Limit Line (NLL) of the Yellow Sea. The NLL served as the maritime border between North and South Korea. The area has seen frequent military drills that have exasperated the situation.

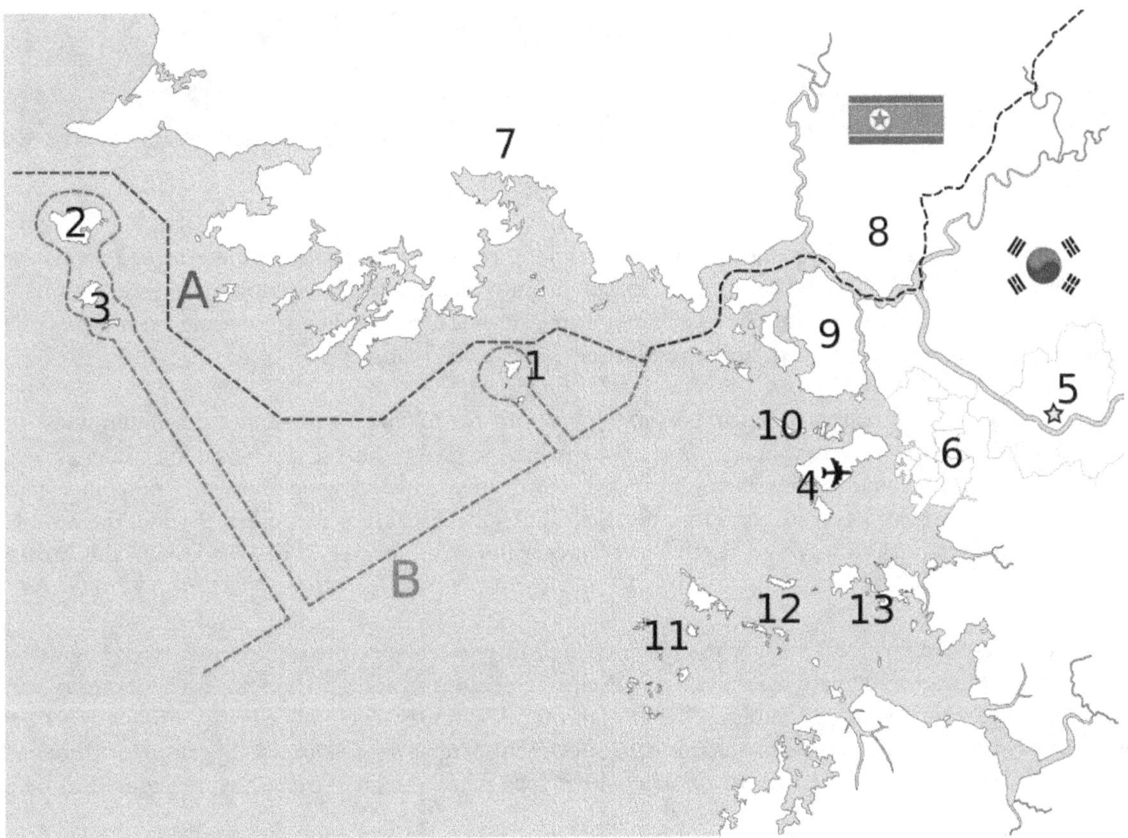

Image/dispute over the Islands of Yeonpyeong[10]

(2) - <u>South-East Asia</u> This part of Asia concentrates on the tensions between China and the intra-ASEAN countries (Indonesia, Malaysia, Brunei, Singapore, Thailand, the Philippines and Vietnam). In post-Cold War South-East Asia, a number of territorial disputes have assumed significance for their potential to disrupt intra-ASEAN relations and regional stability.[11] For instance Malaysia and Singapore are engaged in a dispute over the Pedra Branca island off the coast of Johar which has caused the two countries to put their forces on alert, also the Malaysian and Philippines dispute over the province of Sabah and over maritime boundaries have caused considerable tension, especially in April 1988 when the arrest by the Malaysian Navy of 49 Filipino fisherman who allegedly intruded into Malaysian waters had caused military mobilization by the Philippines. Also other disputes have caused tensions between each other states (Indonesia, Thailand, Brunei, Philippines).[12]

---

[10] https://en.wikipedia.org/wiki/Bombardment_of_Yeonpyeong

[11] Malcolm Chalmers, Confidence-Building in South-East Asia, Westview Press, 1996, p14

Territorial dispute over the Spratly Islands[13]

Spratly Islands and other territories in the South China Sea (West Philippine Sea) – China, Taiwan, Vietnam, Brunei, Malaysia and the Philippines; and a group of islands in the South China Sea could well become the scene of a major dispute involving six or seven Asian nations. [14] In February 1995 tensions had increased when the Philippines's armed forces discovered Chinese-built concrete markers and structures on the tiny islands of Mischief Reef, inside waters claimed by the Philippines. Instantly, it seemed Chinese territory was within 200 kilometers of one of the main Philippine islands, Palawan. The Philippine government retaliated by ordering its air force to destroy the Chinese-built structures. In addition, sixty-two Chinese were arrested by the Philippine navy for fishing within Filipino waters.[15]

These occurrences are the most recent in a sequence of events stretching back to 1974 when Chinese forces seized the Paracel Islands to the north of the Spratly Islands.The Spratly Islands are currently occupied by five nations - Vietnam, the Philippines, Malaysia, Taiwan and China. Brunei also claims Territory. The occupying countries back their claims with military facilities such as airstrips and armed forces on various islands.[16]

The Spratly Islands are already developing into important fishing grounds for China, Vietnam and the Philippines. In addition, there is the possibility of even more valuable resources: oil and gas. New sources of energy for China as well as Vietnam, the Philippines, Malaysia and Indonesia could further power their expanding economies. China, in recent times has become an importer of oil and gas and therefore needs to find substantial new resources. Overall the Spratly Islands region is rich in resources but is also of great strategic value, being at the center of the sea linking the Indian and Pacific Oceans.[17]

Thus these islands have a strategic economic value; for instance a country's territory usually extends twelve nautical miles from its land borders but up to 200 nautical miles as an exclusive economic zone. Inside this area a country can exercise its right to fish and mine while prohibiting other nations. A country claiming islands, no matter how insignificant they appear on maps and navigation charts can effectively extend its resources. It can also influence events in that region - a point not lost on the nations of South-East Asia when military strength is considered to be a valuable asset.[18]

---

[12] Chalmers, op cit:76
[13] Somchai Kongkamsri - https://static.pexels.com/photos/20258/pexels-photo.jpg
[14] Chalmers, op cit:46
[15] Chalmers, op cit:93
[16] Chalmers, op cit:47
[17] Mark J. Valencia, Trouble Waters, The Bulletin of the Atomic Scientists, 1997, p50
[18] Ibid

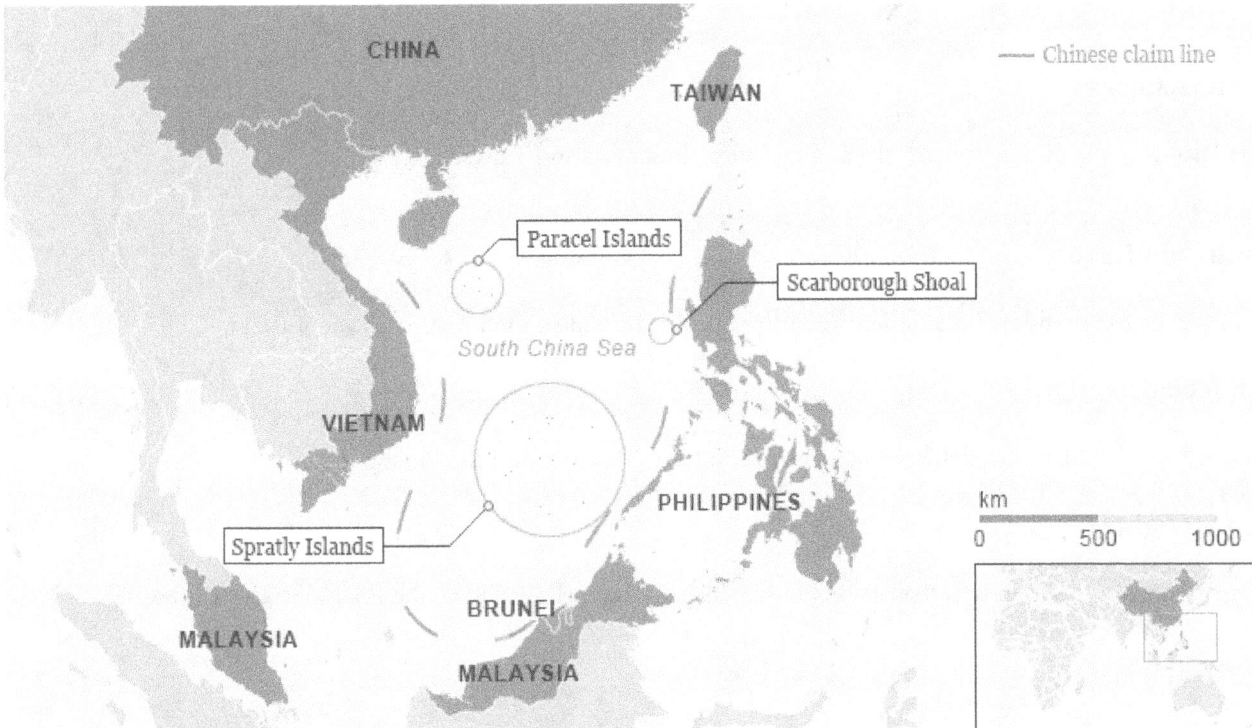

Image/dispute over the Spratly Islands[19]

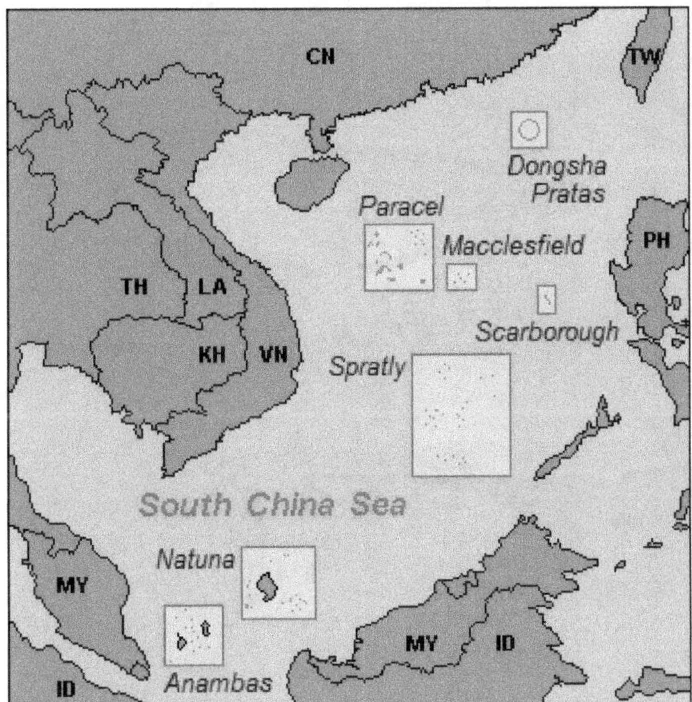

Image/dispute over the South China Sea[20]

Paracel Islands

Paracel Islands in the South China Sea (SCS), which are claimed by China and Vietnam (but occupied by China)[21]

Scarborough Shoal

Scarborough Shoal in the South China, which are claimed by China, Taiwan, and the Philippines.

Pratas Islands

Pratas Islands in the South China, which are claimed by China, Taiwan, and the Philippines.

Macclesfield Bank

Macclesfield Bank in the South China, which are claimed by China, Taiwan, and the Philippines.

---

[19] http://www.dw.com/en/china-installs-weapons-on-disputed-spratly-islands-report/a-3677066

[20] https://commons.wikimedia.org/wiki/File:Karta_CN_SouthChinaSea.PNG

[21] Ben Dolven, Mark Manyin, Shirley Kan, Maritime Territorial Disputes in East Asia: Issues for Congress, CRS Report, 2014

Natuna Islands

Natuna Islands in the SCS, which are claimed by China, Indonesia and Taiwan

Palawan and Luzon

Palawan and Luzon maritime boundaries, which are claimed by China, the Philippines and Taiwan.

Sabah Islands

Sabah and Ambalat Islands, which are claimed by Indonesia, Malaysia, and the Philippines.

Luzon Straight

Maritime boundary and islands in the Luzon Strait, which are claimed by China, the Philippines and Taiwan.[22]

Image/pixabay.com/Hawkeye airborne early warning aircraft

---

[22] Ben Dolven, Mark Manyin, Shirley Kan, Maritime Territorial Disputes in East Asia: Issues for Congress, CRS Report, 2014

Chapter 2: Economic Rivalry

Image/pixabay.com/boat speeding tactical military training

There is also the concern over increasing competition for energy resources, a consequence of increasing rapid East Asian economic growth, is producing growing insecurity in the East Asian region. Some experts think that a major war or serious confrontation could be caused by competition to obtain certain vital resources. The countries in East Asia are dependent on foreign supplies of its increasing energy demand due mainly to the rapid economic growth, thus requiring large amounts of energy in forms such as oil.[23]

For instance petroleum, coal, and natural gas continue to be in insufficient supply in East Asia, countries such as Japan remain 95 percent dependent on oil imports. The growing Chinese economy's hunger for energy has made that country a net oil importer, and increasing demand among other countries in the region will intensify competition for oil supplies and raise insecurity about neighbours' plans to ensure a supply of energy. With the lifeblood of their industries dependent on the increasing traffic of seafaring fleets, East Asian countries have deemed it important to invest in arms build-up, particularly in naval capability, to ensure the safety of unarmed oil-carrying tankers.[24]

Hence, competition for resources is one of the main reasons for increases in tensions in the region – primarily conflict over fishery and energy resources. This conflict has increased due to overfishing in coastal waters that has resulted in fishing boats to go further ashore. In addition, the increase in energy demands for the rising economies in the region has led more to more offshore energy developments in the country's economic planning.

---

[23] Economist, op cit:82
[24] Ibid

Energy and Fishery Resources

The Spratly are thought to hold vast natural resources such as oil and natural gas. It also has vast fishing resources that will help countries in the region supply fishery products locally as well as internationally. The area is also of strategic importance due to its commercial shipping traffic. It has one of the world's busiest maritime trade routes that provide countries with a base to project military force. The regional dispute has been argued by nations such as China, Taiwan and Vietnam on an historical basis. Some countries such as the Philippines claim part of the territory under UNCLOS agreement. This agreement has been ratified by the countries involved in the Spratly dispute.

Oil exploration and continuous dredging by certain countries have increased tensions. For instance, satellite imagery showed China constructing military airfields in the disputed Spratly Islands. Its more assertive approach has begun to cause alarm of its neighbours. They see China attempting to assert its regional hegemony in this region.

The Chinese government ministry has estimated that the South China Sea could contain up to 17.7 billion tons of crude oil. This is significantly more than the estimate crude oil of the Middle Eastern country of Kuwait (estimated at 13 billion). In addition, A US geological survey conducted by Energy Information Administration (EIA) puts the regions discovered and undiscovered natural gas resources between 190 trillion cubic feet to 500 million cubic feet. [25]

Image/pixabay.com/Vietnamese fishermen/fishing boats/offshore oil drilling

United Nations Convention on the Law of the Sea (UNCLOS)

The United Nations Convention on the Law of the Sea (UNCLOS) is an international agreement that came into force in 1994. It is also known as the Law of the Sea Convention or the Law of the Sea Treaty. The previous 'freedom of the seas' concept that had existed since the 17th century had given countries a 3 nautical miles (5.6 km) rights in regards to the countries coastlines. UNCLOS gives the rights and responsibilities of countries in regards to their use of the world's oceans and maritime boundaries. This convention has been joined by 167 countries since 2016. [26]

The multitude of disputes in the region and the inability to agree to frameworks has led to the region spending more on their defence. The increase in defence spending in the region is to dissuade and deter a potential conflict over the areas of interest. In addition, different interpretations of UNCLOS and the unwillingness to submit to dispute settlement procedures have allowed tensions in the region to foster further. UNCLOS allow countries to claim their maritime rights around their sovereign land territory, but does not state who owns which land or landmasses.

---

[25] Ben Dolven, Mark Manyin, Shirley Kan, Maritime Territorial Disputes in East Asia: Issues for Congress, CRS Report, 2014
[26] Ronald O'Rourke, Maritime Territorial and Exclusive Economic Zone (EEZ) Disputes Involving China: Issues for Congress, CRS Report, 2014

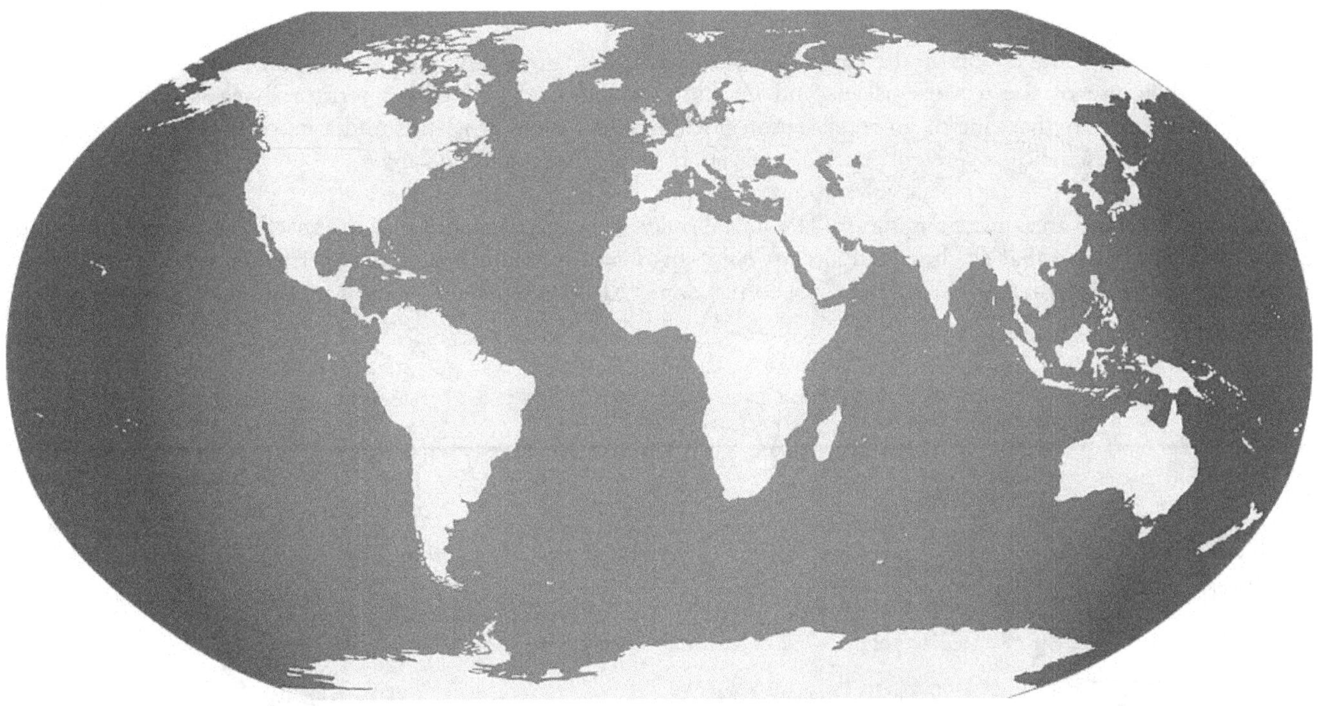

Image/pixabay.com/World map

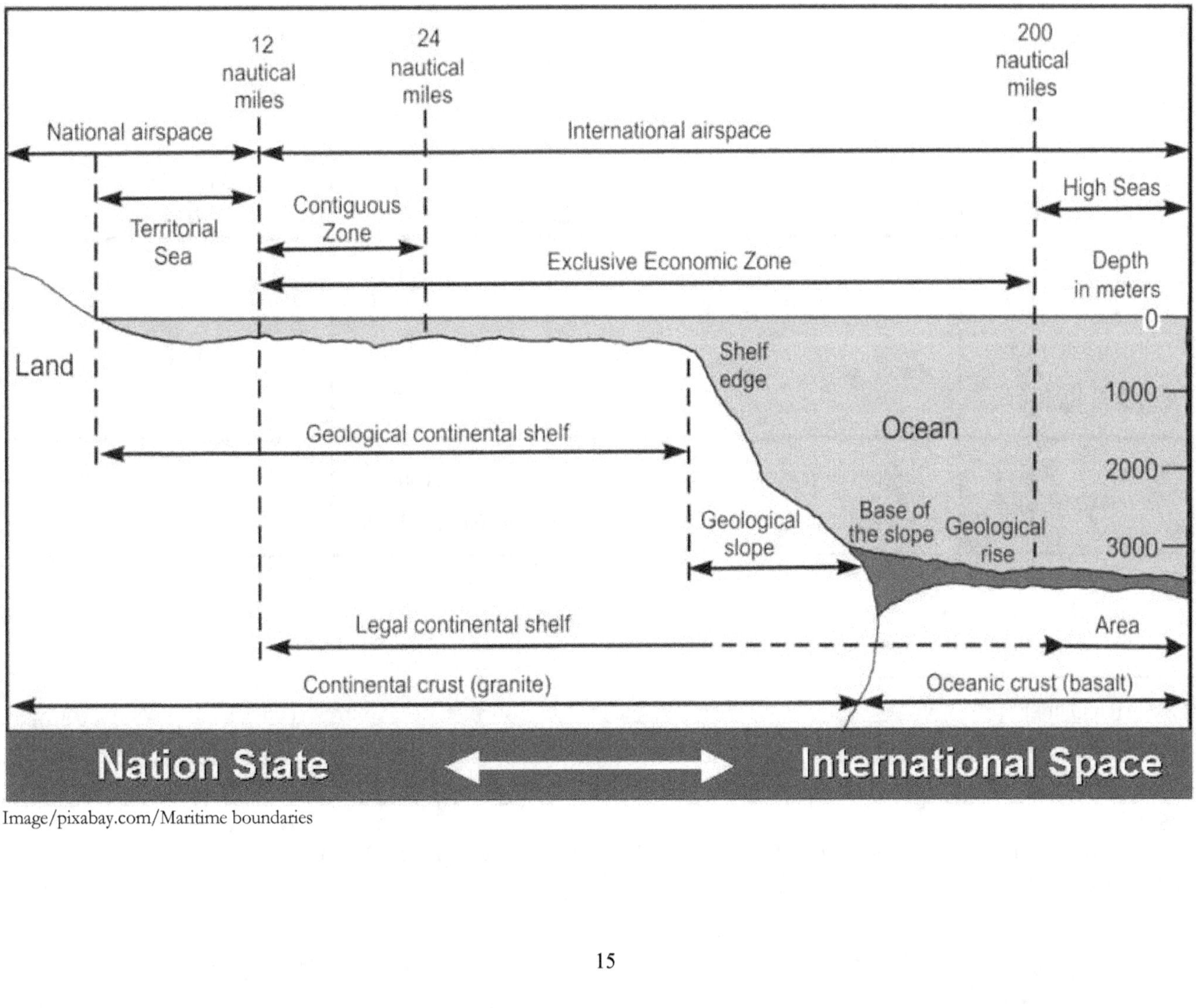

Image/pixabay.com/Maritime boundaries

The United Nations Convention on the Law of the Sea (UNCLOS) gives the rights and responsibilities of countries in regards to their use of the world's oceans and maritime boundaries.[27] UNCLOS territorial sea is given up to 12 nautical miles from the baseline of a coastal nation (including any islets or islands under its control). In this area the countries have full rights of sovereignty such as economic development and policing.[28]

Contiguous Zone are areas extending up to 24 nautical miles in which countries may exercise their sovereignty rights. Some countries believe that all ships and aircraft enjoy high seas freedom (including overflights) but others such as China dispute this interpretation. Exclusive Economic Zone (EEZ) extends up to 200 nautical miles from the nations baseline.

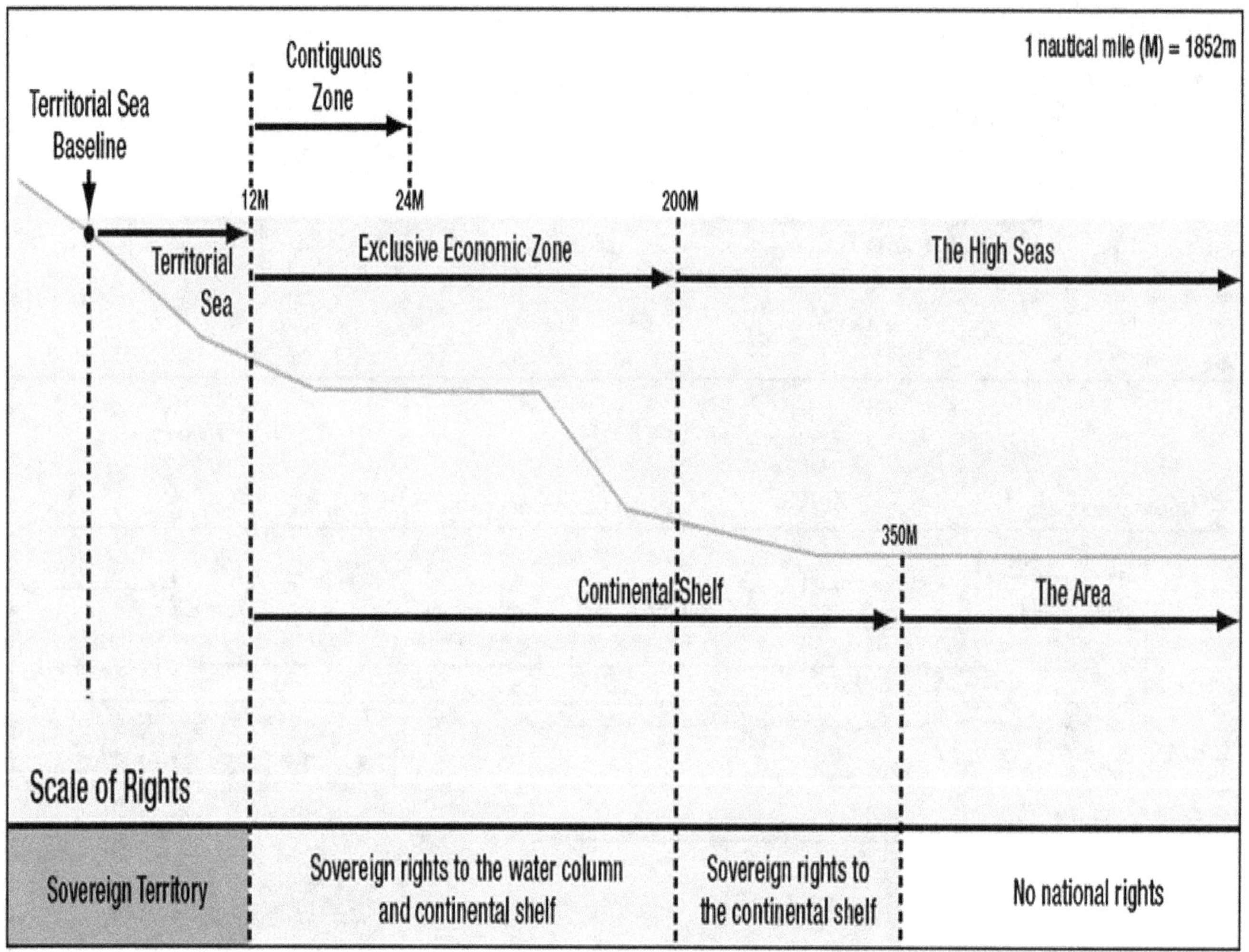

Maritime Boundaries in the UNCLOS. [29]

---

[27] Research Gate -https://www.researchgate.net/figure/Sea-zones-defined-by-the-1982-United-Nations-Convention-on-the-Law-of-the-Sea_302220381

[28] Ronald O'Rourke, Maritime Territorial and Exclusive Economic Zone (EEZ) Disputes Involving China: Issues for Congress, CRS Report, 2014

[29] Arctic Council, *Arctic Marine Shipping Assessment 2009 Report* (Tromsø, Norway: 2009), http://pubs.rsc.org/en/Content/ArticleHtml/2014/NP/c3np70123a

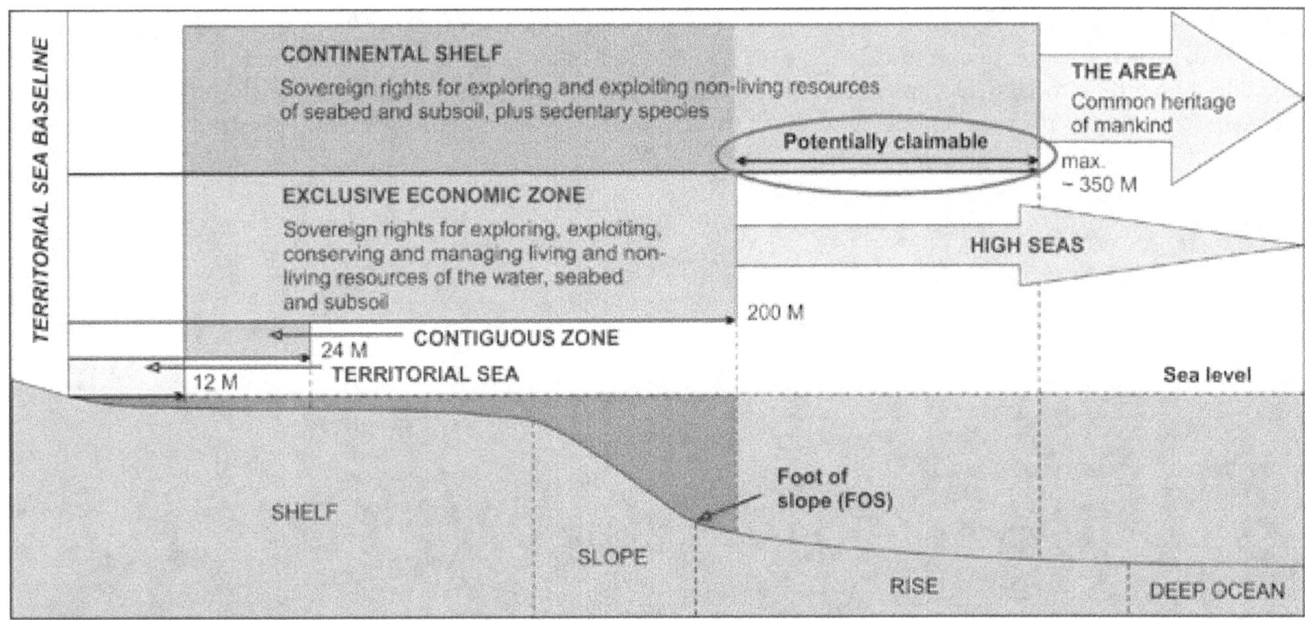

Illustration of maritime zones.[30]

UNCLOS allows all the nations in the area to resolve their dispute. They have all signed up to it, but interpret slightly different if it affects their claim. UNCLOS provides dispute-resolution mechanisms including the International Tribunal of the Law of the Sea (ITLOS) and has the ability to refer disputes to the International Court of Justice (ICG). The drawback is that parties that have signed up to this do not accept its dispute resolution as in the recent case of China. For instance China's claims in the South China Sea are not based on UNCLOS's provisions but rely instead of historical documents predating UNCLOS.[31]

The countries in the East Asian region have in the past relied on different ways to show that they have sovereignty, such as historical administrative control (via occupation or construction of Islands of landmasses). Countries have declared islets which are no more than rocks at high tide as sovereign territories. This claim for islets has led to more aggressive posturers taking amongst rival nation. The following will highlight some of the simmering tensions in the region:

- The increasing frequency of the Sino-Japan incidents in the Senkakus (both claimants trying to demonstrate claims and sovereignty in the area).

- China and Philippines dispute in 2012 of the Scarborough Shoal area.

- China and Vietnam stand off when China's National Offshore oil Corporation moved an oil rig into waters claimed by both nations. This was an attempt to show effective control of the area.

- Five countries occupy parts of the Spratly Islands to demonstrate their administrative control.[32]

---

[30] BGR -
https://www.bgr.bund.de/EN/Themen/Zusammenarbeit/TechnZusammenarb/Projekte/Abgeschlossen/Sektorvorhaben_Ueberregional/101 8_2006-2122-7_Ueberregional_SeerechtskonventionenUNCLOS_en.html?nn=8400038

[31] Ronald O'Rourke, Maritime Territorial and Exclusive Economic Zone (EEZ) Disputes Involving China: Issues for Congress, CRS Report, 2014

[32] Ben Dolven, Mark Manyin, Shirley Kan, Maritime Territorial Disputes in East Asia: Issues for Congress, CRS Report, 2014

UNCLOS allows countries to claim various rights and privileges once sovereignty over an island or rock can be established. An Exclusive Economic Zone up to 200 nautical miles is given to country from its landmass if it is habitable. According to UNCLOS provision, if the landmass is not habitable but extends above the sea level at high tide then it is seen as a rock and entitled to only 12 nautical miles. This is one of the reasons why the many claimant's in the South China Sea have built structurers and bases.[33]

Image/pixabay.com/freedom of the seas/shipping lanes

Economic activities in the region – potential conflict:

The Chinese state owned company, China Offshore Exploration Corp is planning to spend $30 billion in oil exploration within the next 20 years.[34]

Philippines has undertaken oil exploration since the 1970s. A Philippine oil company had discovered an oil field near Palawan Islands close to the South China Sea, which supplies 15% of annual consumption.
The South China Sea has also abundant fishing opportunities that support local and international communities. There have been a number of clashes between the regional members, such as the regular tensions that exist between China and the Philippines.

Chinese troops have clashed with Vietnamese troops over the Paracel Islands. A number of small Islands and reefs are controlled by China, Vietnam, Philippines, Malaysia and Taiwan and each one is trying to consolidate its area under control.

Vietnam has concluded over 60 oil and gas explorations in the region with many foreign companies. It has reached an agreement with Japan on the development of Oil exploration in the South China Sea.

Indonesia has positioned itself as a non-claimant in the South china dispute. However Indonesia's sovereignty over the Natuna Island and nearby area has been seen to overlap China's nine-dash line overlap. The Chinese have argued

---

[33] Ronald O'Rourke, Maritime Territorial and Exclusive Economic Zone (EEZ) Disputes Involving China: Issues for Congress, CRS Report, 2014
[34] Ben Dolven, Mark Manyin, Shirley Kan, Maritime Territorial Disputes in East Asia: Issues for Congress, CRS Report, 2014

that the waters around Natuna are natural fishing grounds which Indonesia has rejected and stated that China has no legal basis here.[35]

Rise of Nationalism

The increasing number of tensions in East Asia has also begun to bring feelings of nationalism to forefront. National pride in the politics of the countries in this region may make it difficult for governments to compromise or negotiate. Increase nationalistic tendencies have been seen in China, Japan, Philippines, South Korea and Vietnam.

Image/pixabay.com/Chinese flag

Image/pixabay.com/A10 Thunderbolt attack aircraft

---

[35] Ben Dolven, Mark Manyin, Shirley Kan, Maritime Territorial Disputes in East Asia: Issues for Congress, CRS Report, 2014

Chapter 3: The Military Build-Up

Image/pixabay.com/US Army AH-64D Apache Helicopters

Introduction

A sharp increase in the military budget of East Asian countries has continued despite the negative impact of the global financial crisis. The nations in this region have procured sophisticated 'state of the Art' weapons, with an emphasis of key 'game changing' items in the region – modern submarines, ships, aircraft and long range anti-ship missiles. For instance, the following purchases have been made:

- China has purchased Su35 Multi-role combat aircraft
- Vietnam is in the process of acquiring Russian Kilo class submarines
- Malaysia is obtaining F18 combat aircraft
- Japan has ordered the F35 Stealth Joint Strike Fighters
- South Korea has purchased the Apache Gunship helicopters
- Australia's purchase of 12 submarines, 100 F-35 Joint Strike Fighters and eight new warships[36]

There is a fear that the region is sliding into an arms race due to the simmering differences amongst themselves. One countries purchase of weapons has given the impetus for a rival to obtained further arms. This increase in regional insecurity in East Asia has resulted in the increase in military expenditure.

---

[36] Chapter six: Asia. (2017). *The Military Balance, 117*(1), 237-350.

Increase in military spending 2016

As the economic development in the region continues, more money has been allocated for safeguarding their respective interests.

Global Military Budget (regional 2016)

Total defence spending in 2016 – 1,504,167 billion
Table 1[37]

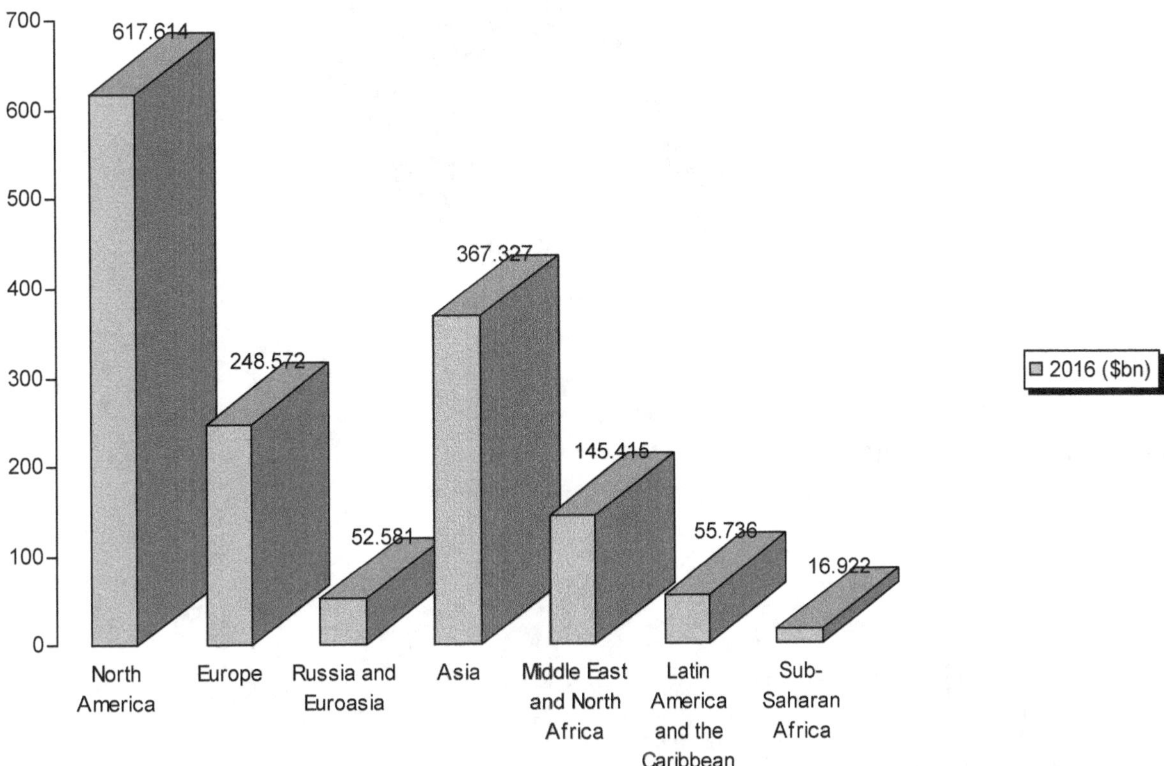

---

[37] Chapter six: Asia. (2017). *The Military Balance, 117*(1), 237-350.

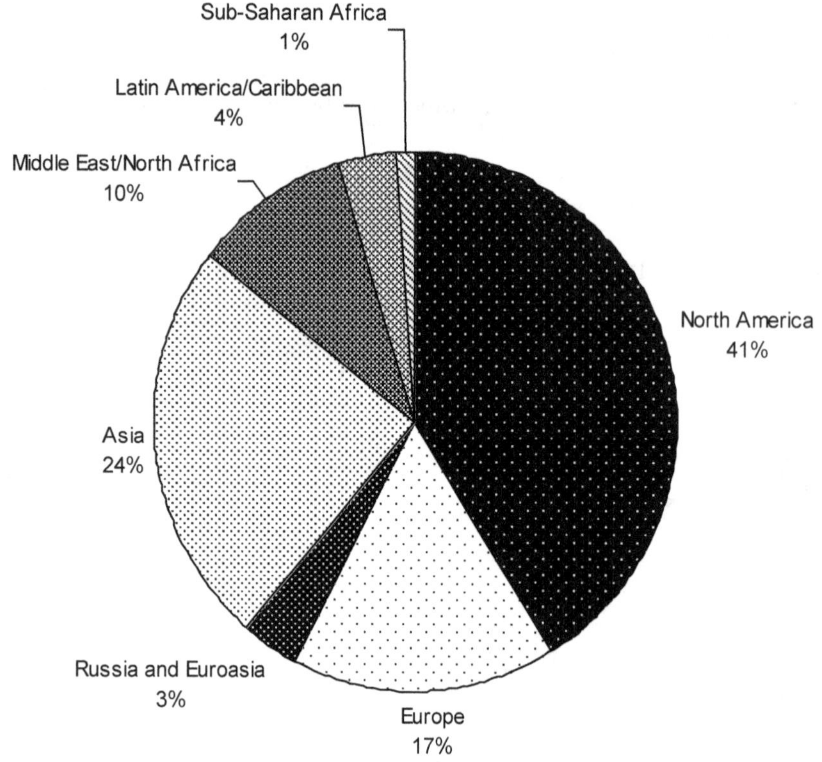

Global Military Budget (% 2016)[38]

Image/pixabay.com/amphibious landings

---

[38] Chapter six: Asia. (2017). *The Military Balance, 117*(1), 237-350.

Defence budgets in East Asia (2016)

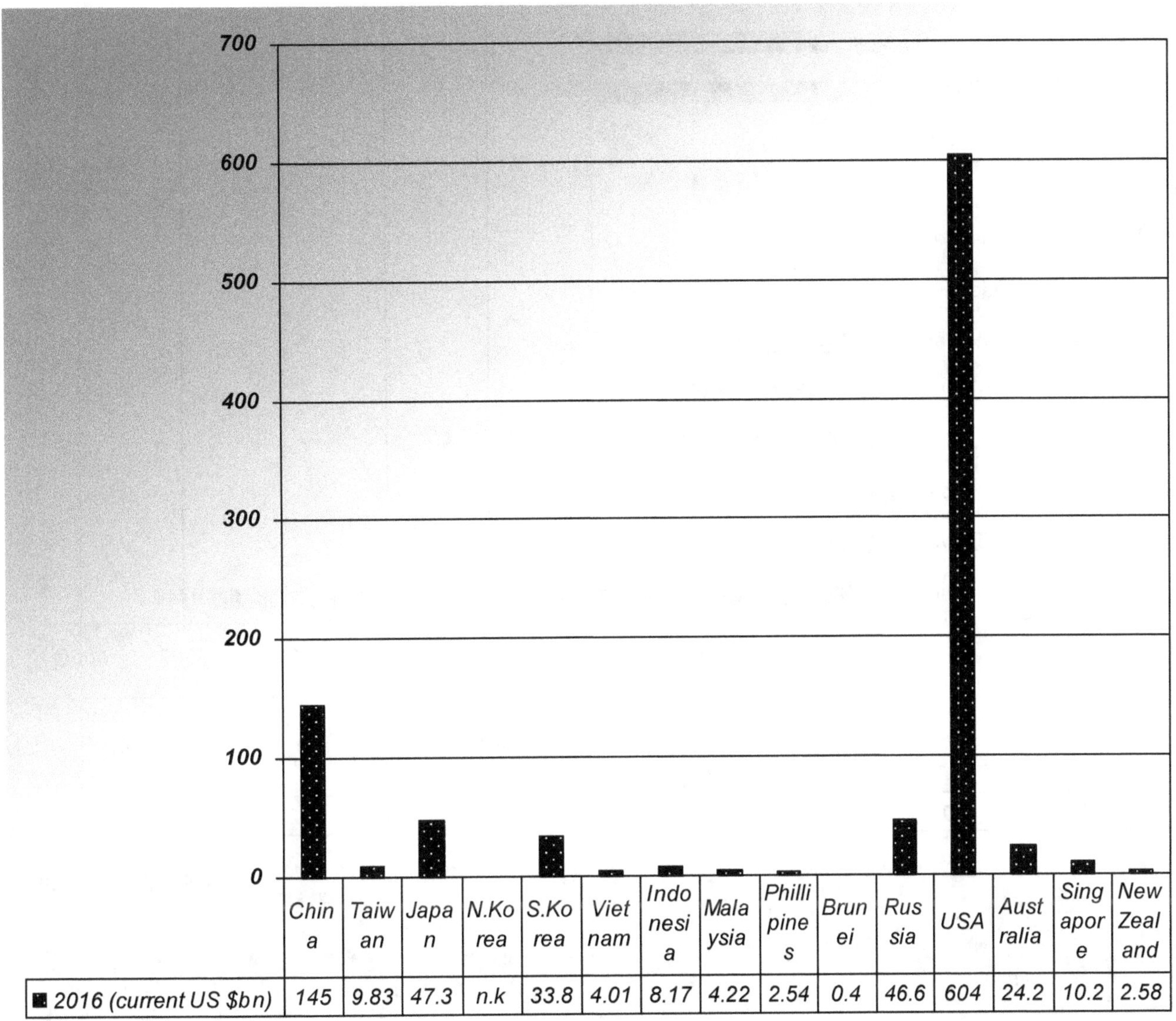

■	Chin a	Taiw an	Japa n	N.Ko rea	S.Ko rea	Viet nam	Indo nesi a	Mala ysia	Philli pine s	Brun ei	Rus sia	USA	Aust ralia	Sing apor e	New Zeal and
2016 (current US $bn)	145	9.83	47.3	n.k	33.8	4.01	8.17	4.22	2.54	0.4	46.6	604	24.2	10.2	2.58

Table 1[39]

Table 2. East Asia's distribution of main battle tanks (MBT), 2016

[39] Chapter six: Asia. (2017). *The Military Balance, 117*(1), 237-350.

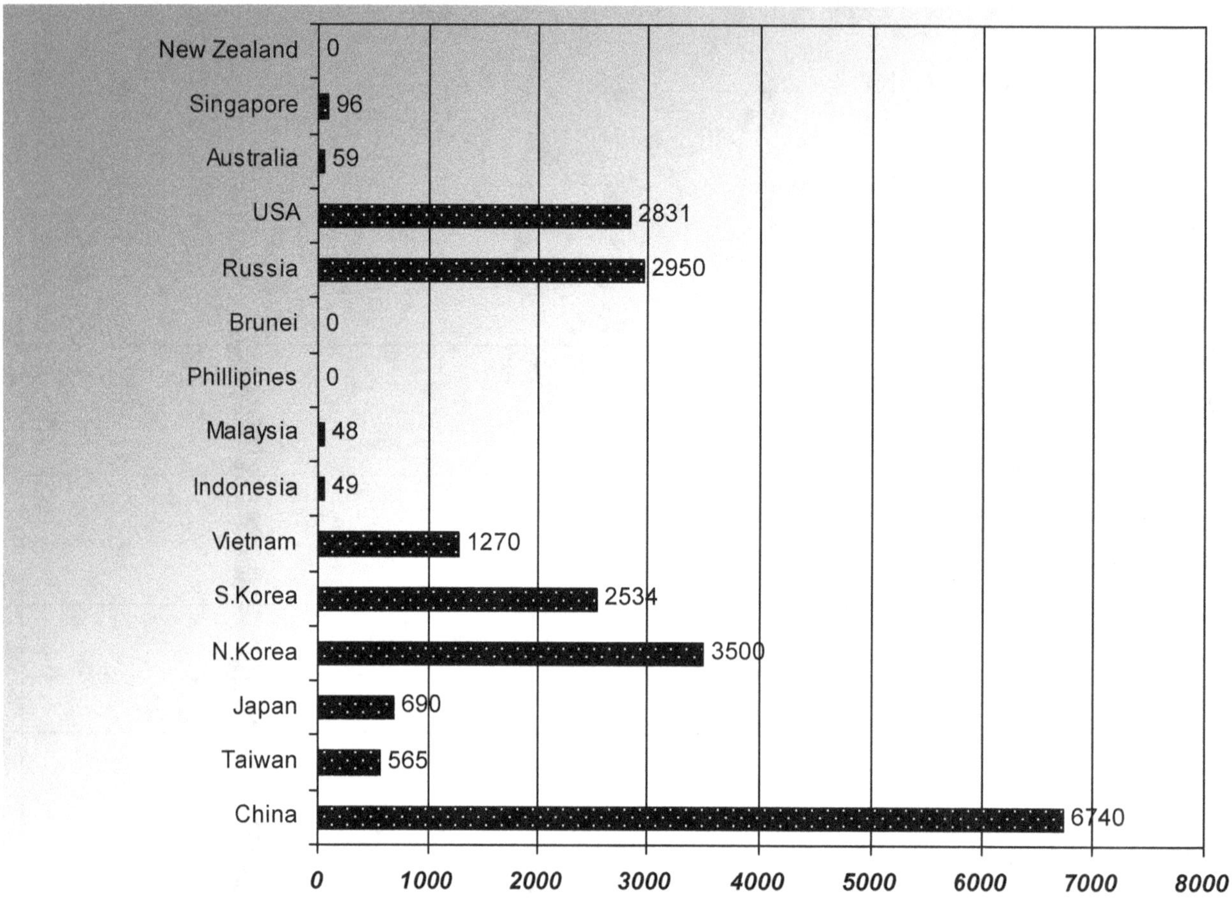

	Chi na	Tai wan	Jap an	N.K ore a	S.K ore a	Viet na m	Ind one sia	Mal aysi a	Phill ipin es	Bru nei	Rus sia	US A	Aust ralia	Sin gap ore	New Zeal and
■ *Main Battle Tank (2016)*	6740	565	690	3500	2534	1270	49	48	0	0	2950	2831	59	96	0

Image/pixabay.com/South Korean Tank

Table 3. East Asia's distribution of combat aircraft, 2016[40]

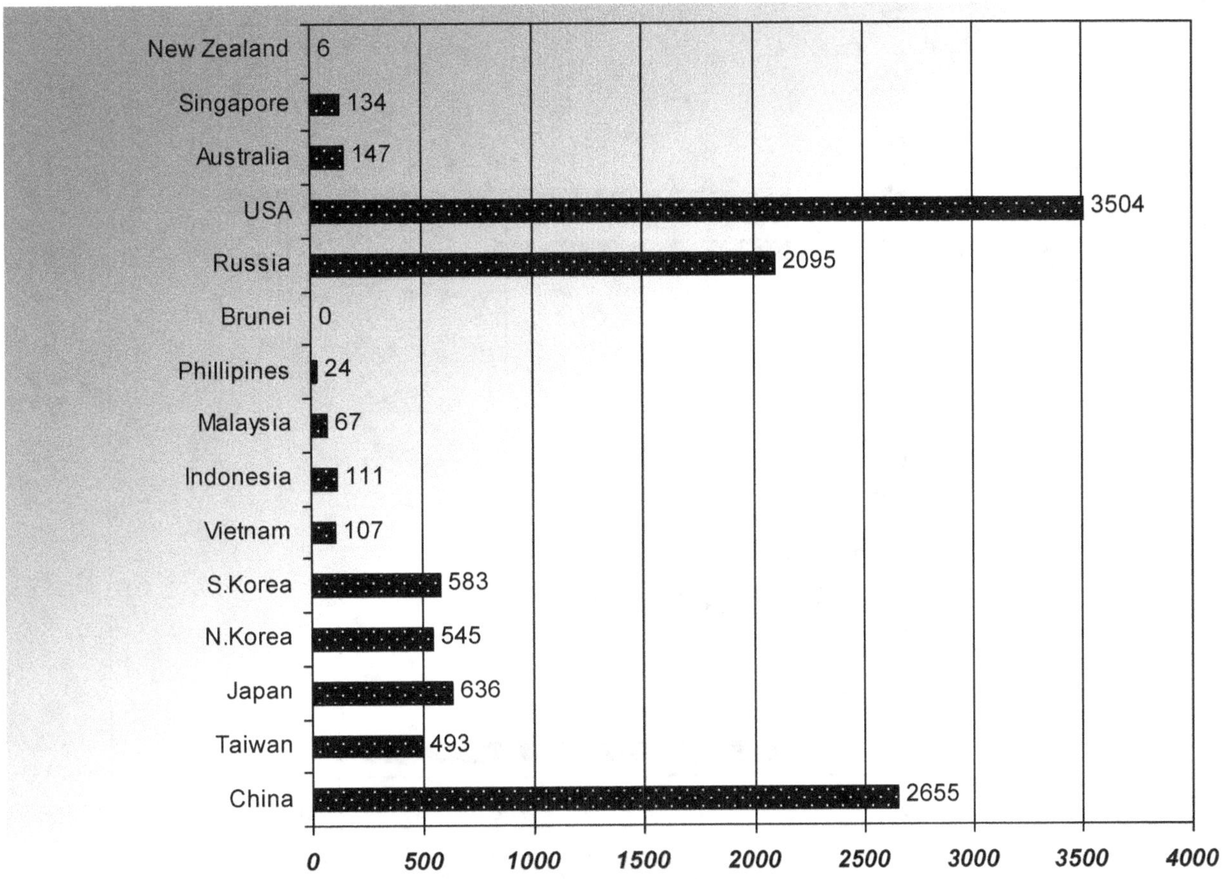

	Chi na	Tai wan	Jap an	N.K ore a	S.K ore a	Viet na m	Ind one sia	Mal aysi a	Phill ipin es	Bru nei	Rus sia	US A	Aust ralia	Sin gap ore	New Zeal and
■ *Combat Aircraft (2016)*	2655	493	636	545	583	107	111	67	24	0	2095	3504	147	134	6

Image/pixabay.com/Combat aircraft

Table 4. East Asia's distribution of principle surface warships and submarines, 2016[41]

---

[40] Chapter six: Asia. (2017). *The Military Balance, 117*(1), 237-350.

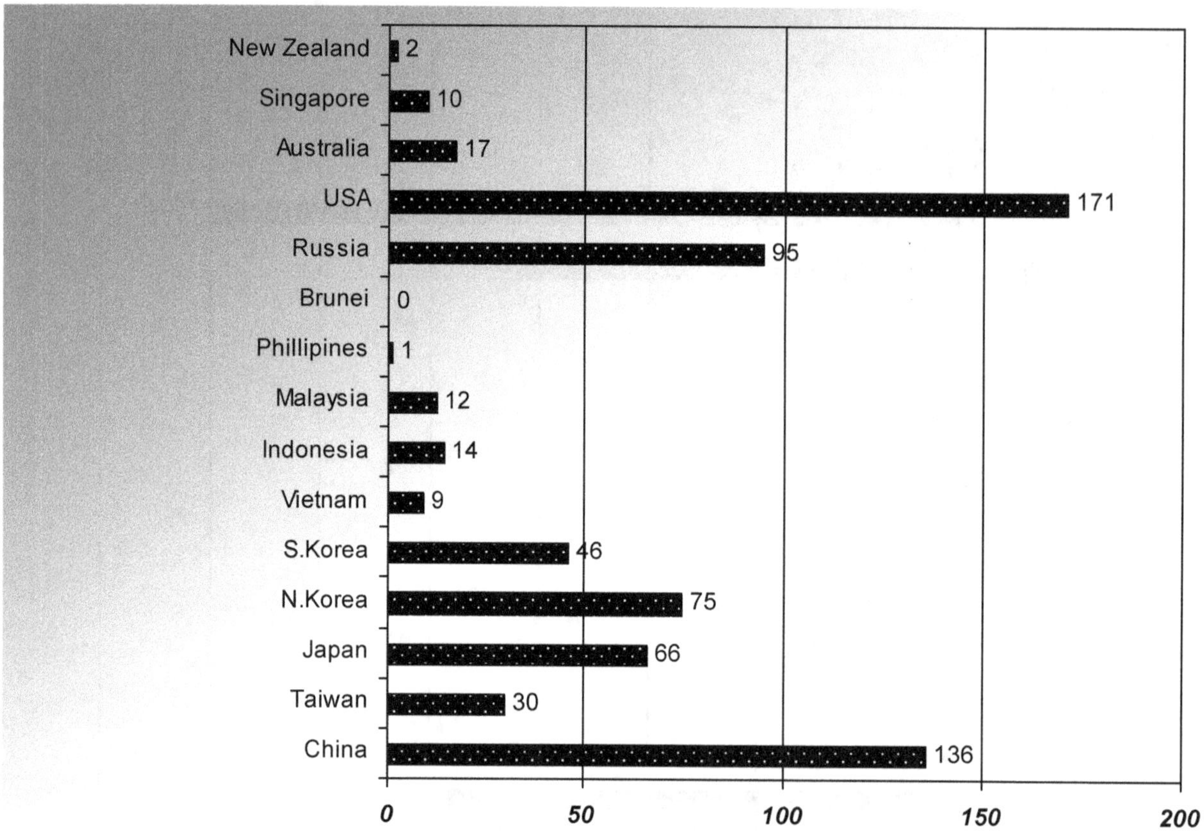

	Chi na	Tai wa n	Jap an	N.K ore a	S.K ore a	Viet na m	Ind one sia	Mal ays ia	Phil lipi nes	Bru nei	Ru ssi a	US A	Aus trali a	Sin gap ore	Ne w Zea
■ *Principle surface warships and Submarines (2016)*	136	30	66	75	46	9	14	12	1	0	95	171	17	10	2

Image/pixabay.com/Warships

---

[41] Chapter six: Asia. (2017). *The Military Balance, 117*(1), 237-350.

Image/pexels.com/M777 Howitzer Artillery

Explanatory Frameworks

Flash Points

There are different reasons and motivations for the countries in East Asia to increase their military budgets. A number of territorial issues, claims made for each nation's respective EEZ zones, sovereignty issues have further exasperated the increase in defence spending. Countries are focusing on strengthening their naval combat and patrol capabilities and updating key areas of their armed forces.

Hedging Strategies

East Asian nations are using a number of strategies such as hedging to deal with the potential threats they face from their rivals. China's rapid economic growth and military upgrade has spurred many other countries to hedge against their security concerns. Hedging against potential threats allows the nations to steadily grow and counter any anticipated military threats.

Many countries in the region have increased their weapon acquisition and have also further cemented their relationship with other major powers that are operating in this region. For instance, South Korea has close military relationship with the USA and sees its partnership with the USA as a counter to stronger powers in the region (such as China).[42]

The China Factor

---

[42] Michael Beckley, The Emerging Military Balance in East Asia: How China's Neighbours Can Check Chinese Naval Expansion, The MIT Press, 2017

The rapid economic rise of China has enabled this country to modernise its armed forces which had numerous obsolete equipment in its inventory. The modern wars in the Middle East, Kosovo and Afghanistan have shown how effective modern weapons with its sophisticated technology can quickly dismantle, subdue and destroy countries (such as the case of Iraq, Afghanistan, Kosovo, Libya, Syria etc.). This had further given the impetus for China to rapidly modernise its obsolete equipment of the early 1980s.

Image/pixabay.com/F-16 combat aircraft

China has a number of potential flash points that could easily escalate in to a military conflict. Sovereignty claims, dispute with renegade Taiwan (separatist threats), EEZ zones of dispute (safe transportation of oil and raw materials), some form of dispute with its neighbours. China is fully aware that some of its neighbours are hedging on some kind of support from the current sole Super Power, the USA and its allies. China is trying to ensure that it reduces the USA's hegemonistic ambitions in this region.[43]

China does not match up to the highly technological sophisticated forces of the US armed forces. China is trying to narrow the gap so that it can deter a potential threat from the US and its allies. The USA is currently supplying very advanced weapons to countries that China has a dispute with, such as Taiwan.
In addition, there is also a national pride in seeing China as a great powerful nation that is not at the 'mercy of its enemies'. The humiliation subjugation of china by Japan and other powers prior to World War 2 has convinced the Chinese that they need to be economically and military strong to ensure that it cannot be colonised as was the case in the past.

It can be argued that China has an insecurity dilemma due its disputes with neighbouring countries, separatist issues that may be inspired by foreign powers, protection of its economic lanes. For china, military modernisation can be seen as a reliable and visible way to deter ethnic and separatist forces and enhance national cohesion. It needs to develop a capability that can cope with an ever changing environment (uncertain war).

China's rapid economic development has allowed the government to devote a bigger share of the rising national revenue to the defence budget. This rise in the increase in Chinese 'firepower' has resulted in other countries in the region to upgrade their militaries.

Regional Security in Transition - Shifting Domestic Politics

US regional hegemony was seen to be eroding since the demise of the Soviet Union. US military commitments in the Iraq, Syria and Afghanistan region had made it focus more in this region and hence slowly eroding its hegemony in East Asia. New challenges, a nuclear North Korea, a more assertive Japan, simmering disputes in the region and the rapid rise of China has now given the US the motivation to reengage and strengthen its forces in the East Asian region.

---

[43] Michael Beckley, The Emerging Military Balance in East Asia: How China's Neighbours Can Check Chinese Naval Expansion, The MIT Press, 2017

A deeper look into East Asia's rise of military expenditure is primarily due to internal changes in some key countries that have affected the regional redistribution of Power in the region. It has made the management of regional conflicts and the prospects of stability more challenging.

China-U.S. Naval Confrontations

China and US confrontation seems to be increasing in regards to the different understanding on UNCLOS and EEZ. US insist that it can patrol in EEZ areas of other countries which China disagrees. A number of potential incidents have increased tensions between these two countries. The US has a much stronger military arsenal consisting of state of the art weapon systems. The Chinese have begun to modernise their military but still have a long way to catch up to the higher technological forces that the US operates.

The US has a number of military pacts with Philippines, South Korea and Japan that requires it to support these countries in the event of a conflict. This commitment could bring the US into direct conflict with China due to the countering claims of its allies in the region. Hence military confrontations are seen to be rising.[44]

The Military Build-Up

The rapid economic growth and the numerous disputes have encouraged military modernisation in the region. Everywhere in East Asia, countries are spending more on their military forces, making this the only region in the world where military expenditures has been rising since the end of the Cold War. The East Asian share of world military expenditure has doubled over the past ten years, defence expenditures in 1992 amounted to some $105 billion and by 1995 this was projected to rise to more than $130 billion, by which time it will be the equivalent of all of Europe (excluding the states of the former Soviet Union). [45]

The rising tensions over border disputes and territorial issues in the South China Sea has exacerbated defence spending in Asia, According to the IISB US$349.1 billion was spent in 2015 and this was increased to US$367.7 billion in 2016. This was an increase of 5-6% each year on defence spending since 2012-16 period. [46]

In continuing this build-up, the nations of East Asia are proceeding according to a long-term blueprint for military modernization. In particular, they are enhancing their capabilities by transforming their existing land-oriented armed forces into modern military establishments with well-equipped air and naval components with a significant capacity to deploy military force at sea and to distant locations.[47]

China began this transformation in 1985, when it adopted a new military doctrine based on possible involvement in regional conflicts on its periphery. Before 1985, Chinese doctrine was focused on the possibility of an all-out 'people's war'-protracted ground combat with the Soviet Union or another invading power. Similarly, other nations in Southeast Asia have begun to convert their land armies-which, until recently, were focused on counterinsurgency operations-into modern forces with integrated armor and artillery units. [48]

They have also sought to enhance power projection by assembling modern air and naval services. Malaysia, Singapore, and Thailand have each established mechanized brigades or divisions equipped with modern tanks and armored personnel carriers, and they are forming 'blue water' navies capable of sustained operations far from port. Indonesia has also expanded its air and naval forces, and it has built up its long-range surveillance and communications capabilities.[49]

---

[44] Michael Beckley, The Emerging Military Balance in East Asia: How China's Neighbours Can Check Chinese Naval Expansion, The MIT Press, 2017
[45] Chalmers, Greene & Zhiqiong, op cit:25
[46] Chapter six: Asia. (2017). *The Military Balance, 117*(1), 237-350.
[47] Ibid
[48] Chalmers, Greene & Zhiqiong, op cit:53

Arms purchases

As they restructure their armed forces, the East Asian nations have become fervent consumers of military hardware produced in the United States, Russia, Britain, France, and other highly industrialized nations. In the period from 1985-94 the region imported weapons valued at $67 billion.[50] By 2016 this region's defence spending had increased to a massive US$367.7 billion in 2016

Some of the major purchases due to the increase in the defence budgets in the region included some of the following 'state of the art' weapons: 26 Su-27 Flankers plus 24 MIG-31 Foxhound fighters and four Kilo-class submarines (China); two AWACS early-warning planes and 36 Multiple-Launch Rocket Systems in addition to 'Patriot' anti-ballistic missile system (Japan); 120 F-16 Falcon fighters and 80 UH-60 Blackhawk helicopters (South Korea); 18 MiG-29 Fulcrums and eight F-18 Hornet fighters in addition to 18 Hawk 200 fighters (Malaysia); 60 Mirage-2000-5 and 150 F-16 Falcon jet fighters (Taiwan); 18 F-16 fighters and three EC-2 Hawkeye airborne early-warning planes (Thailand).[51]

The arms procured in these dealings are often the most sophisticated types obtainable, and they include the latest in fire-control radars, electronic warfare systems, and the like. In addition the wealthier nations of the region also have mounted a significant military-industrial effort by setting up home-based arms factories. Countries such as China, Japan, South Korea, Singapore, Indonesia and Taiwan-have industries capable of building all main types of weapons, such as combat aircraft, helicopters, guided missiles, armoured vehicles, and surface ships.[52]

Military Doctrine

The military arms build-up in the region has the essential components of an integrated, long-range strategic plan. The nations of East Asia are well on their way toward building a large and diversified military-industrial complex. As the East Asian nations increase their defence expenditures and continue to import sophisticated weapons and at the same time expand their arms-making capabilities, their overall military capabilities will constantly improve, as will the threat they pose to their neighbours and rivals. This is the kind of settings in which regional arms races can speed up and spin out of control. There is no sureness that that will occur in East Asia, but the danger is very real. Thus, the rapid economic development has altered the security environment in this part of the world. [53]

Image/pexels.com/warship and B2 Stealth bomber

---

[49] Brown, op cit:103
[50] Michael Klare, East Asia's Militaries Muscle Up, The Bulletin of the Atomic Scientists Publishers, 1997, p56
[51] Brown, op cit:84
[52] Klare, op cit:57
[53] Klare, op cit:58

Image/pexels.com/Cobra Gunship helicopter

Military capabilities, 2017

<u>Northeast Asian Military Forces in 2017</u>

	China	Taiwan	Japan	N. Korea	S. Korea
Population	1,381,306,106	23,464,787	126,702,133	25,115,311	50,924,172
GDP (2016) $bn	11.4tr	519bn	4.73tr	Data not available	1,40tr
Defence budget (2016) $bn	145bn	9.82bn	47.3bn	Data not available	33.8bn
Armed Forces Manpower	2,183,000	215,000	247,150	1,190,000	630,000
Reserves	510,000	1,657,000	56,000	600,000	4,500,000
Main Battle Tank	6,740 (723 LT TK)	565 (625 LT TK)	690	3,500 (560 LT TK)	2,534
AIFV/APC	8,820	1,647	863	2,532+	3,140

Artillery	13,218+	2,254	1,774	21,100+	11,038+
Principal Surface warships	79	26	47	2	23
Submarines	57	4	19	73	23
Combat Aircraft	2,655	493	636	545	583
Armed Helicopters	240	96	104	0	64
Multi-role Helicopters	858	153	386	286	518
Strategic Missiles	533	12	0	70	30

Source: Based primarily on material in the IISS Military Balance 2015-2016, London, Routledge, 2017. Some data estimated or corrected by the author.

Southeast Asian Military Forces in 2017

Image/pixabay.com/mechanized infantry/soldiers training

	Vietnam	Indonesia	Malaysia	Philippines	Brunei

Population	95,261,021	258,316,051	30,949,962	102,624,209	436,620
GDP (2016) $bn	200bn	941bn	303bn	312bn	10.5bn
Defence budget (2016) $bn	4.01bn	8.17bn	4.22bn	2.54bn	402m
Armed Forces Manpower	482,000	395,500	109,000	125,000	7,000
Reserves	5,000,000	400,000	51,600	131,000	700
Main Battle Tank	1,270 (620 LT TK)	49 (415 LT TK)	48 (21 LT TK)	0 (7 LT TK)	0 (20 LT TK)
AIFV/APC	1,680	815	848	491	45
Artillery	3,040+	1,110	424	285+	24
Principal Surface warships	2	12	10	1	0
Submarines	7	2	2	0	0
Combat Aircraft	107	111	67	24	0
Armed Helicopters	26	6	0	11	0
Multi-role Helicopters	44	149	77	86	41
Strategic Missiles	0	0	0	0	0

Source: Based primarily on material in the IISS Military Balance 2015-2016, London, Routledge, 2017. Some data estimated or corrected by the author.

Other Key East Asian Military Forces in 2017

Image/pixabay.com/US army soldiers waiting to board aircraft

	Russia	USA	Australia	Singapore	New Zealand
Population	142,355,415	323,995,528	22,992,654	5,781,728	4,474,549
GDP (2016) $bn	1.27tr	18.6tr	1.26tr	297bn	179bn
Defence budget (2016) $bn	46.6bn	604bn	24.2bn	10.2bn	2.58bn
Armed Forces Manpower	831,000	1,347,300	57,800	72,500	8,950
Reserves	2,000,000	865,050	21,100	312,500	2,200
Main Battle Tank	2950 (17,500 store)	2831 (3500 store)	59	96 (100 store) (372 LT TK)	0
AIFV/APC	14,132 (14,500 store)	14,289	684	2,102	95
Artillery	5281 (4,760	6833	239	798+	74

	store)				
Principal Surface warships	33	103	11	6	2
Submarines	62	68	6	4	0
Combat Aircraft	2095	3504	147	134	6
Armed Helicopters	592	760	22	19	0
Multi-role Helicopters	685	3898	122	51	13
Strategic Missiles	400	540	0	0	0

Source: Based primarily on material in the IISS Military Balance 2015-2016, London, Routledge, 2017. Some data estimated or corrected by the author.

Image/pexels.com/M109 Paladin Howitzer Artillery

Arms Purchases of major weapons (2006-2016)

A look at the major arms acquisition by the nations in East Asia indicates the military build-up. Please note the information is from SIPRI arms transfers from 2006-2016. Transfers of major weapons: Deals with deliveries or orders made for 2006 to 2016. A brief look at each countries purchase of major weapons.

China

Images/pixabay.com/Chinese flag/sailors/J-20 Stealth fighter and Aircraft carrier

The Chinese armed forces, People's Liberation Army (PLA) is one of the fastest growing military force in the world. The PLA currently is the largest military force in the world, consisting of 2,183,000 personnel. It has the second largest defence budget after the USA - $145 billion. The PLA is rapidly modernising its military which consisted primarily of obsolete equipment. Modern warfare and the lessons of the Gulf War, Kosovo, Iraq, Afghanistan has shown the PLA of the capabilities of modern adversaries such as the USA. It is studying tactics on ways of exploiting the vulnerabilities of advanced enemy. It is focusing on asymmetric warfare, network-centric warfare, C4ISR, Sophisticated weaponry and joint operations. The PLA is looking at the ways of using existing military equipment to defeat a technological superior enemy.

By 2017, China had 2,183,000 active duty armed forces and about 510,000 reserves making it the largest military in the world. It has 100,000+ personnel working on strategic missiles (ICBM sites and SLBM). The PLA army numbers 1,150,000 with 510,000 reserves. It has 6,740 MBT and 8,820 IFV/APCs. The navy has 235,000 personnel and 57 submarines and 79 principal surface warships (including 1 aircraft carrier, 21 destroyers and 57 frigates). The Chinese air force has 398,000 personnel with 2,655 combat aircraft (strike and heavy bombers). It has the ability to project powers beyond its immediate area. It has continued to develop and purchase sophisticated state of the art weapons.[54] The table below shows the weapons procured from the period 2006 – 2016.

China's weapon procurement

Source: 2006-2016 SIPRI Arms Transfers Database[55]

Supplier/ recipient (R)	No. ordered	designation	Weapon description	Year(s) Weapon of order	Year delivery	of delivered
Belarus						
R: China	5	Il-76M	Transport aircraft	(2011)	2013	(5)
Second-hand; incl 2 Il-76MD and 3 Il-76TD version; ordered via Russia						
France						
R: China	..	Crotale	SAM system	(1978)	1992-2016	(48)
Chinese designation HQ-7, FM-80 and FM-90; possibly FM-80 and/or FM-90 produced in China are modified Chinese design						
	..	R-440 Crotale	SAM	(1978)	1990-2016	(2275)
Incl R-440N version; Chinese designation HQ-7 (US designation CSA-4 and CSA-N-4); possibly later production in China is modified Chinese design based on R-440 Crotale						

---

[54] The Military Balance, 01/2017, Volume 117, Issue 1

[55] SIPRI Arms Transfers Database - http://armstrade.sipri.org/armstrade/page/trade_register.php

	Weapon designation	Weapon description		Deliveries	
..	AS565S Panther	ASW helicopter	(1980)	1989-2016	(45)

AS-365F version; Chinese designation Z-9C Haitun

| | SA-321 Super Frelon | Transport helicopter | (1981) | 2001-2016 | (55) |

Chinese designation Z-8 (incl Z-8A, Z-8B, Z-8K, Z-8S and Z-8JH versions)

| () | Sea Tiger | Air/sea search radar | (1986) | 1987-2006 | (26) |

For 2 Type-052 (Luhu) and 1 Type-051B (Luhai) destroyers, 2 Type-054 (Jiangkai-1) and 14 Type-053 (Jiangwei1 and Jiangwei-2) and 6 Type-053H1G (Jianghu-5), and 4 Type-071 (Yuzhao) AALS produced in China and for modernization of 2 Type-051 (Luda-2) destroyers; probably incl production (possibly without French licence) in China as Type-360 or Type-363 or SR-60

| | AS365/AS565 Panther | Helicopter | 1988 | 1992-2016 | (417) |

Chinese designation Z-9A or Z-9A-100 Haitun and Z-9B/G; incl Z-9WZ anti-tank version

| (75) | AS-350/AS-550 Fennec | Light helicopter | (1992) | 1995-2011 | (75) |

Chinese designation Z-11; incl Z-11W armed version

| | 12PA6 | Diesel engine | (2000) | 2005-2016 | (100) |

For 2 Type-054 (Jiangkai-1) and 27 or more Type-054A (Jiankai-2) frigates produced in China

| (26) | 16PC2.5 | Diesel engine | (2005) | 2007-2016 | 18 |

PC-2.6 version for 6 Type-071 (Yuzhao) AALS and 1 Danyao support ship produced in China

| | 12PA6 | Diesel engine | (2010) | 2013-2016 | (60) |

For Type-056 (Jiangdao) frigates produced in China

Germany (FRG)

R: China   .. | BF8L | Diesel engine | (1981) | 1982-2016 | (4550)

For YW-531 (Type-63), YW-531H (Type-85), YW-534 (Type-89), YW-535 (Type-90), WZ-551 and WMZ-551 (Type-92) APC (incl IFV and other versions), PLT-02 tank destroyer, PTL-05 self-propelled mortar and Type-85 self-propelled gun produced in China; incl BF-8L4 version

| (18) | MTU-1163 | Diesel engine | (1987) | 1993-2007 | 18 |

For 2 Type-051C (Luzhou), 2 Type-052B and 2 Type-052C (Luyang-1 and Luyang-2), 1 Type-051B (Luhai) and 2 (Type-052) Luhu destroyers produced in China; probably incl assembly or production in China

| (48) | MTU-396 | Diesel engine | (2000) | 2001-2006 | 48 |

For 13 Type-039G (Song) submarines produced in China; probably produced in China

| (8) | MTU-1163 | Diesel engine | (2008) | 2013-2015 | 8 |

MTU-12V-1163 version for 4 Type-051C (Luyang-2) destroyers produced in China

| (28) | MTU-956 | Diesel engine | (2010) | 2014-2016 | (8) |

MTU-20V-956 version for 14 Type-052D (Luyang-3) destroyers produced in China

---

Russia

R: China | (105) | Su-27S/Flanker-B | FGA aircraft | 1996 | 1998-2007 | (105)

Part of $1.5-2.5 b deal for 200 but about 95 cancelled; assembled from kits; Chinese designation J-11

| (1000) | Kh-31A1/AS-17 | Anti-ship missile/ARM | (1997) | 2001-2016 | (1000) |

Kh-31A and Kh-31P or Kh-31AMK and Kh-31PMK version; for Su-30, J-8M and/or JH-7 combat aircraft; including production of Kh-31P in China as KR-1, YJ-9 or YJ-91

| (1500) | 9M119 Svir/AT-11 | Anti-tank missile | (1998) | 2001-2015 | (1500) |

For Type-98 and Type-99 tanks; possibly produced or copied in China as GP7 from 2015 or technology used in development of GP7

| 4 | Fregat/Top Plate | Air search radar | (2001) | 2004-2007 | 4 |

For 2 Type-051C (Luzhou) and 2 Type-052B (Luyang-1) destroyers produced in China; probably produced (possibly without license) in China

| (105) | AK-630 30mm | Naval gun | (2002) | 2004-2016 | (105) |

For 2 Type-054 (Jiangkai-1) frigates, over 80 Type-022 (Houbei) FAC and 4 Type-071 (Yuzhao) AALS produced in China and 4 Zubr landing craft from Ukraine; probably produced in China

| | AK-176 76mm | Naval gun | (2004) | 2008-2016 | (23) |

Chinese-produced H/PJ-26 version for 27 or more Type-054A (Jiangkai-2) frigates produced in China

| | Mineral/Band Stand | Sea search radar | (2004) | 2008-2016 | (23) |

For 27 or more Type-054A (Jiangkai-2) frigates produced in China; probably produced (possibly without license) in China

| (6) | AK-176 76mm | Naval gun | (2005) | 2007-2016 | 4 |

Chinese-produced H/PJ-26 version for 6 Type-071 (Yuzhao) AALS produced in China

| (18) | Mineral/Band Stand | Sea search radar | (2008) | 2013-2016 | (7) |

For 4 Type-052C (Luyang-2) and 14 Type-052D (Luyang-3) destroyers produced in China; probably produced (possibly without license) in China

| | AK-176 76mm | Naval gun | (2010) | 2013-2016 | (30) |

Chinese-produced H/PJ-26 version for Type-056 (Jiangdao) frigates produced in China

No.	Designation	Description	Order	Delivery	Delivered
(150)	Kh-59ME Ovod/AS-18	ASM	(1999)	2004-2006	(150)

Incl for Su-30 combat aircraft

6	Mineral/Band Stand	Sea search radar	(1999)	2004-2007	6

For 2 Type-052B (Luyang-1), 2 Type-052C (Luyang-2) and 2 Type-051C (Luzhou) destroyers produced in China

(750)	RVV-AE/AA-12 Adder	BVRAAM	(2000)	2002-2009	(750)

For Su-27SK and Su-30MKK combat aircraft

(150)	3M-54 Klub/SS-N-27	Anti-ship MI/SSM	2002	2005-2009	(150)

For modernized Project-877 and new Project-636 (Kilo) submarines; probably incl 3M14E land-attack version

(150)	48N6/SA-10D Grumble	SAM	(2002)	2006-2007	(150)

For Type-051C (Luzhou or Shenyang) destroyers

(150)	53-65 533mm	AS torpedo	(2002)	2005-2006	(150)

For Project-636 (Kilo) submarines

(200)	9M311/SA-19	SAM	(2002)	2005-2006	(200)

For Kashtan AD system on Project-956EM (Sovremenny) destroyers

(150)	9M38/SA-11	SAM	(2002)	2005-2006	(150)

9M38M1 (SA-N-7) version; for Type-956EM (Sovremenny or Hangzhou) destroyers

(30)	Moskit/SS-N-22	Anti-ship missile	(2002)	2005-2006	(30)

For Sovremenny (Hangzhou) destroyers

(100)	PMK-2	Naval mine/torpedo	(2002)	2004-2007	(100)
8	Project-636E/Kilo	Submarine	2002	2004-2006	(8)

$1.5-2 b deal

2	Project-956/Sovremenny	Destroyer	2002	2005-2006	2

$1-1.5 b deal; Type-956EM version; option on 2 more not used

2	S-300FM/SA-N-20	Naval SAM system	(2002)	2006-2007	2

For 2 Type-051C (Luzhou or Shenyang) destroyers produced in China

(150)	TEST-71	AS/ASW torpedo	(2002)	2005-2006	(150)

For Type-636 (Kilo) submarines

(297)	48N6E2/SA-10E	SAM	2004	2007-2008	(297)
	Fregat/Top Plate	Air search radar	(2004)	2008-2016	(24)

For 27 or more Type-054A (Jiangkai-2) frigates and 1 Liaoning aircraft carrier produced in China; probably produced (possibly without license) in China

(200)	Kh-59MK/AS-18MK	Anti-ship missile	(2004)	2008-2015	(200)

For Su-30 combat aircraft; probably Kh-59MK2 version developed for and funded by China

	MR-90/Front Dome	Fire control radar	(2004)	2008-2016	(92)

For 27 or more Type-054A (Jiangkai-2) frigates produced in China; for use with HHQ-16 SAM; possibly produced in China

8	S-300PMU-2/SA-20B	SAM system	2004	2007-2008	(8)

$980 m deal

(100)	AL-31	Turbofan	2005	2006-2009	(100)

AL-31FN version for J-10 combat aircraft produced in China

(54)	Mi-8MT/Mi-17	Transport helicopter	(2005)	2007-2012	(54)

Mi-171 or Mi-171E version; possibly assembled in China from kits

(750)	48N6E2/SA-10E	SAM	2006	2008-2009	(750)

For S-300PMU-2 (SA-20B) SAM system

9	Ka-27PL	ASW helicopter	(2006)	2009-2010	9

Ka-28PL version

9	Ka-31	AEW helicopter	(2006)	2010-2011	9
24	Mi-8MT/Mi-17	Transport helicopter	2006	2006-2007	24

$200 m deal; probably Mi-171 and/or Mi-17V-5 and/or Mi-17V-7 version

8	S-300PMU-2/SA-20B	SAM system	2006	2008-2009	(8)
(122)	AL-31	Turbofan	2009	2010-2012	(122)

AL-31FN version for J-10 combat aircraft produced in China

55	D-30	Turbofan	2009	2009-2012	(55)

For H-6K bomber aircraft produced in China and possibly for modernization of Il-76 transport aircraft

32	Mi-8MT/Mi-17	Transport helicopter	2009	2010-2011	(32)

Mi-171E version; possibly for incl police or other non-military government agency

4	MR-123/Bass Tilt	Fire control radar	(2009)	2013-2014	2

For 4 Zubr landing craft from Ukraine

123	AL-31	Turbofan	2011	2012-2014	(123)

$500 m deal; AL-31FN version for J-10 combat aircraft produced in China

(150)	AL-31	Turbofan	2011	2012-2016	(80)

AL-31F version for J-15 combat aircraft produced in China

(184)	D-30	Turbofan	2011	2012-2016	(164)

For H-6K bomber aircraft and Y-20 transport aircraft produced in China and modernization of Il-76 transport aircraft

(5)	Il-76M	Transport aircraft	2011	2013-2015	(5)

Second-hand

52	Mi-8MT/Mi-17	Transport helicopter	2012	2012-2014	(52)

Mi-171E version; possibly for incl police or other non-military government agency

(10)	AL-41F	Turbofan	2015	2016	(2)

AL-41F-1S version; spares for Su-35 combat aircraft

(7)	Il-76M	Transport aircraft	(2015)	2015-2016	(7)

Second-hand but probably modernized before delivery

(6)	S-400/SA-21	SAM system	2015		

$3 b deal; delivery possibly from 2017

24	Su-35	FGA aircraft	2015	2016	4

$2 b deal; Su-35S version; delivery 2016-2018

Switzerland

R: China

..	GDF 35mm	AA gun	(1995)	1997-2016	(360)

Chinese designation Type-90 and Type-99

..	Skyguard	Fire control radar	(1995)	1997-2016	(180)

For use with GDF 35mm (Type-90) AA guns and possibly HQ-7 (FM-80) SAM systems

---

Ukraine

R: China

(12)	DT-59	Gas turbine	(1998)	2004-2007	12

For 2 Type-052B (Luyang-1), 2 Type-052C (Luyang-2) and 2 Type-051C (Luzhou) destroyers produced in China; probably DA-80 version; probably incl production in China; probably ordered in several batches

	DT-59	Gas turbine	(2008)	2013-2016	(16)

For 4 Type-052C (Luyang-2) and 14 Type-052D (Luyang-3) destroyers produced in China; DA80/DN80 version produced in China as QC-280

2	Zubr/Pomornik	ACV/landing craft	2009	2013-2014	2

$315-319 m deal incl 2 produced in China; Project-958 Bizon version

(2000)	R-27/AA-10	BVRAAM	(1995)	2000-2009	(2000)

For Su-27SK and Su-30MKK combat aircraft; incl R-27ER (AA-10C) and R-27ET (AA-10D) version

1	Kuznetsov	Aircraft carrier	1998	2012	1

Second-hand (production stopped 1992 with end of Soviet Union and unfinished ship sold 1998 in $20-30 m deal to China officially for static civilian use but finished to modified design for Chinese navy after delivery to China); Chinese designation Type-001 and Liaoning

(42)	AI-25	Turbofan	(2004)	2005-2009	(42)

For JL-8 (K-8) trainer aircraft produced in China

50	6TD	Diesel engine	2011	2013-2014	(50)

Probably for tank produced in China

(250)	AI-222	Turbofan	2011	2016	(20)

$380m deal; AI-222-25F version for L-15 trainer/combat aircraft produced in China

(3)	Il-78M	Tanker/transport ac	2012	2014-2016	(3)

Second-hand but probably modernized before delivery; $45 m deal

---

United Kingdom

R: China

..	Spey	Turbofan	(1975)	1998-2016	(300)

For JH-7 combat aircraft produced in China

Uzbekistan

R: China

3	Il-76M	Transport aircraft	2014	2015-2016	(3)

Second-hand (but modernized in Russia before delivery); Il-76MD version

---

Taiwan

Images/pixabay.com/Taiwan flag/combat aircrafts

The Taiwanese (Republic of China - ROC) has increased its military spending. It has purchased sophisticated weaponry in light of the tensions with China and in the region. The ROC armed forces number 215,000 personnel with reserve forces totaling 1,657,000. Its defence budget is $9.82 billion.

By 2017, Taiwan army numbers 130,000 with 1,500,000 reserves. It has 565 MBT (plus 625 Light Tanks) and 1,647 AIFV/APCs. The navy has 40,000 personnel (67,000 reserves) and 4 submarines and 26 principal surface warships (including 4 cruisers and 22 frigates). The Taiwanese air force has 45,000 personnel (90,000 reserves) with 495 combat aircraft (multi-role strike aircraft).[56] It has continued to develop and purchase sophisticated state of the art weapons in light of the tensions in the region. The table below shows the weapons procured from the period 2006 – 2016. Transfers of major weapons: Deals with deliveries or orders made for 2006 to 2016[57]

Taiwan's weapon procurement

Source: SIPRI Arms Transfers Database

Supplier/ recipient (R)	No. ordered	designation	Weapon description	Year(s) Weapon of order	Year delivery	of delivered
Germany (FRG)						
R: Taiwan (ROC)	90	MTU-4000	Diesel engine	2007	2009-2011	(90)
$149 m deal; for 30 KH-6 FAC produced in Taiwan						
	(24)	MTU-4000	Diesel engine	(2011)	2014	(2)
For 12 Tuo Jiang corvettes produced in Taiwan						
Italy						
R: Taiwan (ROC)	6	Gaeta	MCM ship	2014		
Incl 5 produced in Taiwan; delivery from 2019						
	(12)	Super Rapid 76mm	Naval gun	(2011)	2014	1
For 12 Tuo Jiang corvettes produced in Taiwan						
United States						
R: Taiwan (ROC)	11	TPS-77	Air search radar	2002	2004-2006	(11)
Incl 4 AN/TPS-117						
	54	AAV-7A1	APC	2003	2005-2006	(54)
$64-156 m deal; Second-hand AAV-7A1 rebuilt to AAV-7A1RAM/RS; incl 4 CP and 2 ARV version						
	182	AIM-9L/M Sidewinder	SRAAM	2003	2005-2006	(182)
$17 m deal; AIM-9M-2 version						
	4	Kidd	Destroyer	(2003)	2005-2006	4
Second-hand; $740 m deal; Taiwanese designation Keelung						
	(22)	RGM-84L Harpoon-2	Anti-ship MI/SSM	(2003)	2005-2006	(22)
RGM-84L Block-2 version; for Kidd (Keelung) destroyers						
	(148)	Standard Missile-2MR	SAM	(2003)	2005-2006	(148)
SM-2MR Block-3A version; for Kidd (Keelung) destroyers						

---

[56] The Military Balance, 01/2017, Volume 117, Issue 1
[57] SIPRI Arms Transfers Database - http://armstrade.sipri.org/armstrade/page/trade_register.php

No.	Designation	Description	Order	Delivery	Delivered
(449)	AGM-114K HELLFIRE	Anti-tank missile	(2004)	2007-2008	(449)

Part of $50 m deal; AGM-114M3 version

No.	Designation	Description	Order	Delivery	Delivered
5	AIM-7M Sparrow	BVRAAM	2005	2007	(5)

Part of $280 m deal; for training in USA

| 10 | AIM-9L/M Sidewinder | SRAAM | 2005 | 2006 | (10) |

Part of $280 m deal; AIM-9M version; for training in USA

| (650) | C-9 | Diesel engine | (2005) | 2014-2016 | (605) |

For 650 CM-32 APC/IFV produced in Taiwan

| 1 | FPS-115 Pave Paws | Air search radar | 2005 | 2013 | 1 |

Part of $1.4 b 'SRP' programme

| (218) | AIM-120C AMRAAM | BVRAAM | (2007) | 2013-2014 | (218) |
| 2 | Osprey | Minehunter | (2007) | 2012 | 2 |

Second-hand but modernized before delivery; $30 m deal; Taiwanese designation Yung Jin

| 12 | P-3CUP Orion | ASW aircraft | (2008) | 2012-2015 | (12) |

$664 m deal (offsets 70%); second-hand P-3C rebuilt to P-3CUP

| (32) | RGM-84L Harpoon-2 | Anti-ship MI/SSM | (2008) | 2013-2016 | (32) |

UGM-84L version for Zwaardvis (Hai Lung) submarines; delivery

| 60 | RGM-84L Harpoon-2 | Anti-ship MI/SSM | 2008 | 2010-2012 | (60) |

$90 m deal; AGM-84L Block-2 version; for F-16 combat aircraft

| (144) | Standard Missile-2MR | SAM | 2008 | 2010-2012 | (144) |

SM-2 Block-3A version

| (235) | AGM-65 Maverick | ASM | 2009 | 2011-2012 | (235) |

AIM-65G2 version

| 182 | FGM-148 Javelin | Anti-tank missile | 2009 | 2011 | (182) |

$21-29 m deal

| 171 | FIM-92 Stinger | Portable SAM | 2009 | 2012-2014 | (171) |

$45 m deal; for AH-64E combat helicopters

| (25) | FIM-92 Stinger | Portable SAM | 2009 | 2012 | (25) |

$9.9 m deal; Stinger Block-1 version

| 264 | MIM-104F PAC-3 | ABM | 2009 | 2011-2014 | (264) |

Part of $3.2 b deal

| 4 | Patriot PAC-3 | SAM/ABM system | 2009 | 2014-2015 | (4) |

$1.1 b deal (incl $134 m for spares; part of $3.2 b deal)

| 3 | Patriot PAC-3 | SAM/ABM system | 2009 | 2011-2012 | (3) |

$600 m deal; Taiwanese Patriot SAM systems rebuilt to Patriot-3 version

| (1000) | AGM-114K HELLFIRE | Anti-tank missile | (2010) | 2012-2014 | (1000) |

AGM-114L version for AH-64E combat helicopters

| 30 | AH-64D Apache | Combat helicopter | (2010) | 2012-2014 | (30) |

$2 b deal; AH-64E version

| (17) | APG-78 Longbow | Combat heli radar | (2010) | 2012-2014 | (17) |

For AH-64E combat helicopters

(122)	MIM-104F PAC-3	ABM	(2010)	2015	(122)
(2)	Patriot PAC-3	SAM/ABM system	(2010)		
(9)	T-700	Turboshaft	2010	2013-2014	(9)

Spares for AH-64E combat helicopters

| (12) | Mk-15 Phalanx | CIWS | (2011) | 2014 | 1 |

For 12 Tuo Jiang corvettes produced in Taiwan

| 4 | S-70/UH-60L | Helicopter | 2011 | 2014 | (4) |

UH-60M version; $49 m deal

| (45) | S-70/UH-60L | Helicopter | (2012) | 2014-2016 | (22) |

UH-60M version; delivery 2014-2019

| 144 | APG-83 SABR | Combat ac radar | (2014) | | |

For modernization of 144 F-16 combat aircraft; delivery from 2017

| 2 | AAQ-33 Sniper | Aircraft EO system | 2015 | | |
| 36 | AAV-7A1 | APC | (2015) | | |

Probably second-hand

| 769 | BGM-71F TOW-2B | Anti-tank missile | (2015) | | |

BGM-71F TOW-2B ARF version; selected but not yet ordered by end-2016

| 208 | FGM-148 Javelin | Anti-tank missile | (2015) | | |

Selected but not yet ordered by end-2016

| 250 | FIM-92 Stinger | Portable SAM | 2015 | | |

Selected but not yet ordered by end-2016

| 13 | Mk-15 Phalanx | CIWS | (2015) |
| 2 | Perry | Frigate | (2015) |

Second-hand but probably modernized before delivery; $175-190 m deal; delivery 2017-2018

| (140) | AIM-9X Sidewinder | SRAAM | (2016) |

Japan

Images/pixabay.com/Japanese flag/combat aircrafts and helicopter

The Japanese armed forces (Japan Self-Defence Force JSDF) are a modern sophisticated and extremely capable military force. It has a large defence budget - $47.3 billion. By 2017, Japan had 257,150 active duty personnel and about 56,000 reserves making it a strong military in the East Asian region. The Japanese army numbers 150,850 with 46,000 reserves. It has 690 MBT and 1,774 AIFV/APCs. The navy has 45,350 personnel (8,100 reserves) and 19 submarines and 47 principal surface warships (including 3 aircraft carrier, 2 cruisers, 33 destroyers and 9 frigates).

The Japanese air force has 46,950 personnel (1,100 reserves) with 636 combat aircraft (air defence/attack). It has continued to develop and purchase sophisticated state of the art weapons.[58] The table below shows the weapons procured from the period 2006 – 2016.

Japan's weapon procurement

Source: SIPRI Arms Transfers Database[59]

Supplier/ recipient (R)	No. ordered	Weapon designation	Year(s) description	Weapon of order	Year delivery	of delivered
Australia						
R: Japan	4	Bushmaster	APC	2014	2014	4
AUD3.6 m deal						
France						
R: Japan	..	MO-120-RT 120mm	Mortar	1989	1990-2016	(453)
Incl for Type-96 mortar carrier produced in Japan						
	(14)	Ocean Master	MP aircraft radar	1996	2004-2007	(14)
For 14 US-2 (US-1AKai) MP aircraft produced in Japan						
Germany (FRG)						
R: Japan	(15)	EC135	Light helicopter	2009	2009-2015	(15)
For training; Japanese designation TH-135						
Italy						
R: Japan	5	Compatto 127mm	Naval gun	(1999)	2003-2006	5
For 5 Takanami frigates produced in Japan						
Sweden						
R: Japan	36	Stirling AIP	AIP engine	2005	2009-2016	28
For 9 Souryo submarines produced in Japan; delivery 2009-2018						

---

[58] The Military Balance, 01/2017, Volume 117, Issue 1

[59] SIPRI Arms Transfers Database - http://armstrade.sipri.org/armstrade/page/trade_register.php

United Kingdom

R: Japan	(34)	Spey	Gas turbine	(1991)	1995-2006 · 34

Spey SM1C version for 5 Takanami and 9 Murasame frigates, 1 Kashima training and 2 Mashuu support ships produced in Japan

	12	Type-2093	MCM sonar	(1995)	1999-2007 · 12

For 12 Sugashima MCM ships produced in Japan

	(14)	EH-101-400	Transport helicopter	2003	2006-2016 · (9)

$518 m 'MCH-X' programme; 13 assembled from kits; incl 3 CH-101 transport version (for use in Antarctica) and 11 MCH-101 MCM version (with MCM system from USA)

	16	Spey	Turbofan	2007	2012-2014 · 16

Spey SM1C version for 4 Akizuki frigates produced in Japan

	4	Air refuel system	Air refuel system	2003	2008-2010 · 4

For 4 KC-767 tanker/transport aircraft from USA

	1	Air refuel system	Air refuel system	2009	2010 · 1

For modification of 1 C-130H transport aircraft to KC-130H tanker/transport version

	3	Air refuel system	Air refuel system	2015	

For 3 KC-767 (KC-46A) tanker/transport aircraft from USA

United States

R: Japan		CH-47D Chinook	Transport helicopter	1984	1986-2016 · (103)

CH-47J and CH-47JA version; incl production in Japan

	29	T55-L	Turboshaft	1984	1987-2015 · (29)

T55-K-712 version; spares for CH-47 helicopters

	(70)	LM-2500	Gas turbine	(1988)	1993-2015 · 66

For 2 Hyuga and 2 Izumo helicopter carriers, 4 Kongou and 2 Atago destroyers, 5 Takanami and 9 Murasame frigates and 1 Asuka research ship produced in Japan

	(67)	S-70/UH-60L	Helicopter	1988	1990-2013 · (67)

UH-60J (S-70A-12) version

	27	SeaVue	MP aircraft radar	1992	1995-2010 · 27

For 27 BAe-125-800/RH-800 (U-125A) MP aircraft from UK and USA; Japanese designation APQ-2

	(350)	AIM-7M Sparrow	BVRAAM	1993	1996-2006 · (350)

For Murasame and Takanami frigates; RIM-7M Sea Sparrow (SAM) version

	(99)	M-270 MLRS 227mm	Self-propelled MRL	1993	1995-2006 · (99)
	21	BAe-125-800	Light transport ac	1995	1998-2010 · 21

'H-X' programme; RH-800 or Hawker-800 version; modified in Japan for SAR; Japanese designation U-125A

	(80)	S-70/UH-60L	Helicopter	1995	1998-2016 · (39)

$2.7 b deal; UH-60JA version

	(74)	S-70B/SH-60B Seahawk	ASW helicopter	1997	2005-2016 · (49)

SH-60K version

	(13)	AH-64D Apache	Combat helicopter	2001	2006-2016 · (13)

'AH-X' programme; AH-64DJP version; most assembled in Japan; original plan for up to 62 reduced to 13 for financial reasons

	2	Mk-45-4 127mm	Naval gun	2003	2007-2008 · 2

For 2 Atago destroyers produced in Japan

	(80)	APG-63	Combat ac radar	(2004)	2007-2015 · (80)

AN/APG-63(V)1 version for modernization of F-15J combat aircraft

	(700)	RIM-162 ESSM	SAM	2004	2008-2016 · (650)

For Hyuga helicopter carriers and Akizuki, Takanami and Murasame frigates

	(36)	RIM-161 SM-3 Block-1	SAM/ABM	(2006)	2007-2010 · (36)

Part of $6.5-9.3 b anti-ballistic missile defence system (incl production of components in Japan); SM-3 Block-1A version; for Kongou destroyers

	(40)	S-70/UH-60L	Helicopter	(2010)	2013-2016 · (6)

JPY190 b ($2.3 b) programme; UH-60J version; for SAR

	42	F-35A JSF	FGA aircraft	(2012)	2016 · (1)

USD10 b 'F-X' programme (for 42 incl first 4 ordered 2012 for $756 m)

	(150)	Bell-412	Helicopter	2015	

JPY193 b ($1.6 b) 'UH-X' programme; Bell-412EPI version; delivery from 2021

	3	KC-46A	Tanker/transport aircraft	2015	

$520 m deal (incl production of components in Japan); delivery from 2020

	(110)	F110	Turbofan	(1987)	2000-2012 · (110)

F110-GE-129 version for 94 F-2 combat aircraft produced in Japan (incl spare engines)

No. ordered	Designation	Description	Year of order	Delivery	No. delivered
(38)	Mk-15 Phalanx	CIWS	(1993)	1996-2007	(38)

For 2 Improved Kongou destroyers, 9 Murasame and 5 Takanami frigates and 3 Oosumi AALS produced in Japan; incl some Block-1B version

(56)	AE-2100	Turboprop	(1996)	2007-2016	24

For 14 US-2 (US-1AKai) MP aircraft produced in Japan; AE-2100J version

5	Mk-41	Naval SAM system	(1998)	2003-2006	5

For 5 Takanami destroyers produced in Japan

(13)	APS-145	AEW radar	2000	2004-2008	(13)

For modernization of 13 E-2C AEW&C aircraft to Hawkeye-2000

(13)	APG-78 Longbow	Combat heli radar	2001	2006-2016	(13)

For AH-64D (AH-64DJP) combat helicopters

2	Mk-41	Naval SAM system	(2002)	2007-2008	2

For 2 Atago destroyers produced in Japan

6	SPG-62	Fire control radar	(2002)	2007-2008	6

For 2 Atago destroyers produced in Japan; for use with Standard SAM

2	SPY-1D	Air search radar	2002	2007-2008	2

For 2 Atago destroyers produced in Japan

(150)	FIM-92 Stinger	Portable SAM	(2003)	2006-2009	(150)

AIM-92 version; for AH-64D combat helicopters

4	KC-767 GTTA	Tanker/transport ac	2003	2008-2010	4

'KC-X' programme; KC-767J version

2	Mk-41	Naval SAM system	(2004)	2009-2011	2

For 2 Hyuga helicopter carriers produced in Japan

(64)	Standard Missile-2MR	SAM	(2004)	2006	(64)

SM-2 Block-3B version

(25)	AIM-120C AMRAAM	BVRAAM	(2005)	2006	(25)

AIM-120C5 version

(32)	MIM-104F PAC-3	ABM	2005	2006-2007	(32)

Part of $6.5-9.3 b anti-ballistic missile defence system

40	Standard Missile-2MR	SAM	(2005)	2007	(40)

SM-2 Block-3B version

44	Standard Missile-2MR	SAM	(2006)	2008	(44)

$70 m deal; SM-2 Block-3B version

(6)	King Air	Light transport ac	(2007)	2008-2009	(6)

King Air-90 version; for training; Japanese designation TC-90

8	Mk-15 Phalanx	CIWS	(2007)	2012-2014	8

For 4 Akizuki frigates produced in Japan; Block-1B version

4	Mk-41	Naval SAM system	(2007)	2012-2014	4

For 4 Akizuki frigates produced in Japan

4	Mk-45-4 127mm	Naval gun	(2007)	2012-2014	4

For 4 Akizuki frigates produced in Japan

(24)	Standard Missile-2MR	SAM	2008	2010	(24)

$40 m deal; SM-2 Block-3B version

(348)	GMLRS	Guided rocket	(2009)	2010-2014	(348)
(524)	JDAM	Guided bomb	(2010)	2006-2013	(524)
30	TH-28/480	Light helicopter	2010	2011-2015	(30)

Enstom-480B version; Japanese designation TH-480B; for training

(11)	AQS-24	MCM sonar	2011	2014-2016	(4)

For EH-101 (MCH-101) MCM helicopter from UK

4	SeaRAM	SAM system	2011	2015	2

For 2 Izumo helicopter carriers produced in Japan

13	Standard Missile-2MR	SAM	2011	2014	(13)

$33 m deal; SM-2 Block-3B version

(5)	F135	Turbofan	(2012)		

Spares for F-35A combat aircraft

6	KC-130H Hercules	Tanker/transport ac	(2012)	2014-2016	(6)

Second-hand but modernized before delivery; $170 m deal; KC-130R version

4	ScanEagle	UAV	2012	2013	4

JPY1.2 b ($9.9 m) deal

(6)	T56	Turboprop	2012	2014	6

Second-hand T56A-16 version but modernized before delivery; spares for C-130 transport aircraft

(52)	AAV-7RAM/RS	APC	(2013)	2014	4

(1)	Mk-41	Naval SAM system	(2013)			
For 1 improved Akizuki frigate produced in Japan						
1	AAQ-33 Sniper	Aircraft EO system	2014			
(17)	AIM-120C AMRAAM	BVRAAM	(2014)	2016	(17)	
$33 m deal; AIM-120C7 version						
4	Caterpillar-3126	Diesel engine	2014	2014	4	
For 4 Bushmaster APC from Australia						
(100)	RIM-116A RAM	SAM	(2014)	2015	(50)	
For SeaRAM SAM system on 2 Izumo helicopter carriers						
3	RQ-4A Global Hawk	UAV	(2014)			
Selected but not yet ordered by end-2014; delivery from 2019						
	AIM-9X Sidewinder	SRAAM	2015			
(4)	E-2D Hawkeye	AEW&C aircraft	2015			
Delivery from 2018						
(17)	V-22 Osprey	Transport ac/helicopter	2015			
	RIM-161D SM-3 Block-2	SAM/ABM	(2016)			
2	SPY-1F	Air search radar	2016			
For 2 Improved Atago destroyers produced in Japan						

North Korea

Images/pixabay.com/North Korean flag

The North Korean armed forces (Korean People's Army - KPA) have one of the largest militaries in the world. Its main adversaries are South Korea and the USA and hence it keeps a strong military to deal with these threats. By 2017, North Korea had 1,190,000 active duty armed forces and about 600,000 reserves making it one of the largest military in the world. It has undertaken a number of nuclear tests and is developing long range missiles, such as the Hwasong 14 (KN-04) ICBM. The North Korean army numbers 1,020,000 with 600,000 reserves. It has 3,500 MBT (plus 560 Light Tanks) and 2,532+ AIFV/APCs. The navy has 215,000 personnel and 73 submarines and 2 principal surface warships (including 2 frigates).

The North Korean air force has 110,,000 personnel with 545 combat aircraft (air defence and attack aircraft). It has the ability to project powers beyond its immediate area.[60] KPA operates a large amount of equipment, bust of it is deemed obsolete. North Korea has placed thousands of artillery pieces along the Korean Demilitarized zone. In the event of a conflict this would entail enormous amount of casualties and damage to South Korea. This is one of the main deterrence to other nations, such as the USA of launching an attack. The table below shows the weapons procured from the period 2006 – 2016.

North Korean's weapon procurement

Source: SIPRI Arms Transfers Database[61]

Supplier/ recipient (R)	No. ordered	Weapon designation	Weapon description	Year(s) Weapon of order	Year delivery	of delivered

---

[60] The Military Balance, 01/2017, Volume 117, Issue 1
[61] SIPRI Arms Transfers Database - http://armstrade.sipri.org/armstrade/page/trade_register.php

Russia
R: North Korea   (3000)   9M111 Fagot/AT-4   Anti-tank missile   (1987)   1992-2010   (3000)
Continuation of original order from Soviet Union; status uncertain (probably production of unauthorized copy in North Korea from early-2000s)
                    (1500)   Igla-1/SA-16   Portable SAM   (1989)   1992-2009   (1500)
Probably continuation of original order from Soviet Union
                    (10)   Kh-35 Uran/SS-N-25   Anti-ship missile   (2005)   2006   (10)

South Korea

Images/pixabay.com/South Korean flag/F-15 Eagle combat aircraft/UH-60 Black Hawk helicopters and AH64D Apache Attack helicopter

The South Korean Armed forces (ROK) are a formidable modern military that are geared primarily to deter any North Korean invasion. The Armed forces number 630,000 personnel with 4,500,000 reserves. It has a defence budget of $33.8 billion. By 2017, the South Korean army numbers 495,000 with large reserves. It has 2,534 MBT and 3,140 AIFV/APCs. The navy has 70,000 personnel and 23 submarines and 23 principal surface warships (including 3 cruisers, 6 destroyers and 14 frigates).

The South Korean air force has 65,000 personnel with 583 combat aircraft (multi-role strike aircraft).[62] It has the ability to project powers beyond its immediate area. It has continued to develop and purchase sophisticated state of the art weapons. The table below shows the weapons procured from the period 2006 – 2016.

South Korean's weapon procurement

Source: SIPRI Arms Transfers Database[63]

Supplier/ recipient (R)	ordered	No. designation	Weapon description	Year(s) Weapon of order	Year delivery	of delivered
Canada						
R: South Korea	(105)	PT6	Turboprop/turboshaft	(1995)	2000-2007	(105)
For 85 KT-1 trainer and 20 KO-1 combat/reconnaissance aircraft produced in South Korea; PT-6A-62A version						
France						
R: South Korea	4	16PC2.5	Diesel engine	(2002)	2007	4
For 1 Dokdo (LPX) AALS produced in South Korea						
	66	Crotale-NG	SAM system	2003	2006-2009	(66)
EUR470 m deal; for Chun Ma (Pegasus) SAM system produced in South Korea (with South Korean missiles and chassis)						
	214	EC155	Helicopter	2015		
LCH-LAH version						

---

[62] The Military Balance, 01/2017, Volume 117, Issue 1
[63] SIPRI Arms Transfers Database - http://armstrade.sipri.org/armstrade/page/trade_register.php

(5)	AS365/AS565 Panther	Helicopter	(2002)	2003-2006	5
1	Vampyr	Air search system	(2003)	2007	1

For 1 Dodko (LPX) AALS produced in South Korea

3	Vampyr	Air search system	(2005)	2008-2012	3

Vampyr-MB version; for 3 Sejong the Great (KDX-3) destroyers produced in South Korea

2	Falcon-2000	Light transport ac	(2011)		

Falcon-2000S version for modification in South Korea to SIGINT aircraft; delivery 2017

8	FLASH	ASW sonar	2013	2016	(8)

For 8 AW-159 helicopters from UK

Germany (FRG)

R: South Korea (1740)	MTU-871	Diesel engine	(1981)	1984-2009	(1740)

For 1484 K-1 tanks and 256 K-1 chassis from USA

3	Type-214	Submarine	2000	2007-2009	3

$1.1 b 'KSS-2' programme (incl $711 m components from FRG)

6	Type-214	Submarine	2008	2014-2016	(3)

'KSS-2' programme; delivery 2014-2019

(1306)	MTU-881	Diesel engine	(1998)	1999-2016	(985)

For K-9 self-propelled guns and K-10 ALV produced in South Korea

(36)	MTU-1163	Diesel engine	(2005)	2008-2015	(36)

For 18 Gumdoksuri (PKX-A or PKG-A) FAC produced in South Korea

(400)	MIM-104A Patriot	SAM	(2007)	2008-2012	(400)

Second-hand

(8)	Patriot	SAM system	(2007)	2008-2009	(8)

Second-hand; $370-494 m deal (part of $1-1.2 b 'SAM-X' programme)

(100)	MTU-883	Diesel engine	2012	2014-2015	(100)

For 100 K-2 tanks produced in South Korea; possibly produced in South Korea

(177)	Taurus KEPD-350	ASM	2013	2016	(60)

For F-15K combat aircraft; chosen after USA refused AGM-158; KEPD-350K version

90	Taurus KEPD-350	ASM	(2016)		

For F-15K combat aircraft; KEPD-350K version; selected but not yet ordered by end-2016

Israel

R: South Korea (60)	EL/M-2032	Combat ac radar	2009	2013-2016	(60)

For some 60 FA-50 combat aircraft produced in South Korea

2	EL/M-2080 Green Pine	Air search radar	2009	2012	2

For use with Patriot SAM systems in AMD-Cell air defence/ABM system

(4)	SandCat Spike-NLOS	SSM launcher	2011	2013	4
(67)	Spike-NLOS	SSM/ASM	2011	2013	67

Spike-NLOS Mk-5 version; for ground-based launcher

(60)	Spike-NLOS	SSM/ASM	2013	2016	(60)

Spike-NLOS Mk-5 version; for AW-159 helicopters

3	Heron	UAV	(2015)	2016	(3)

KRW30 b deal

Netherlands

R: South Korea (1)	MW-08	Air search radar	(2003)	2007	1

For 1 Dokdo (LPX) AALS produced in South Korea

5	Goalkeeper	CIWS	2003	2007-2012	5

$54 m deal; for 1 Dokdo (LPX) AALS and 3 KDX-3 destroyers produced in South Korea

1	SMART	Air search radar	2003	2007	1

For 1 Dokdo (LPX) AALS produced in South Korea

Russia

R: South Korea (2000)	9M131 Metis-M/AT-13	Anti-tank missile	2002	2003-2006	(2000)

Part of $534 m 'Bul-Gom' or 'Red Bear-2' deal (incl $267 m debt payment)

(37)	BMP-3	IFV	2002	2005-2006	(37)

Part of $534 m 'Bul-Gom' or 'Red Bear-2' deal (incl $267 m debt payment)

23	Il-103	Light aircraft	2002	2005-2006	(23)

$9 m deal (incl $4.5 m debt payment); part of $534 m 'Bul-Gom' or 'Red Bear-2' deal (incl $267 m debt payment); for training

3	Murena/Type-1206	ACV/landing craft	2002	2005-2006	3

Part of $534 m 'Bul-Gom' or 'Red Bear-2' deal (incl $267 m debt payment)

(10)	T-80U	Tank	2002	2005-2006	(10)

Part of $534 m 'Bul-Gom' or 'Red Bear-2' deal (incl $267 m debt payment)

Spain

R: South Korea 4	A-330 MRTT	Tanker/transport ac	2016		

'KC-X' programme; delivery 2017-2019

Sweden

R: South Korea 18	CEROS-200	Fire control radar	2005	2008-2015	(18)

For 18 Gumdoksuri (PKX or PKG-A) FAC produced in South Korea

6	ARTHUR	Arty locating radar	2007	2009-2010	(6)

$120 m deal

(10)	ARTHUR	Arty locating radar	2011	2013-2015	(10)

$70 m deal

United Kingdom

R: South Korea 1	MT-30	Gas turbine	2012		

For 1 FFX-II frigate produced in South Korea

8	AW-159 Wildcat	ASW helicopter	2013	2016	8
(8)	Trent-700	Turbofan	2016		

For 4 A330 MRTT tanker /transport aircraft from Spain

United States

R: South Korea (256)	K-1 chassis	Tank chassis	1989	1993-2006	(256)

For 56 K-1 ABL (developed in cooperation with UK company) and 200 K-1 ARV (developed in cooperation with FRG company) version

(484)	K-1A1	Tank	(1994)	1999-2009	(484)

KRW1 tr ($781 m) deal; incl 2 or 3 prototypes

67	AAV-7A1	APC	2000	2001-2006	(67)

$99-120 m deal; South Korean designation KAAV (Korean Armoured Amphibious Vehicle)

8	F110	Turbofan	(2001)	2005-2008	(8)

Spares for F-15K combat aircraft

40	F-15E Strike Eagle	FGA aircraft	2002	2005-2008	(40)

$4.2 b 'F-X' programme (offsets 65-83% incl production of components for 32 F-15K and all production of AH-64 combat helicopter fuselages in South Korea); F-15K Slam Eagle version

2	LCAC	ACV/landing craft	(2005)	2007	2

South Korean designation LSF-2

(75)	AAV-7A1	APC	2006	2006-2010	(75)

KRW149 b ($157 m) deal; South Korean designation KAAV (Korean Armoured Amphibious Vehicle)

4	Boeing-737 AEW&C	AEW&C aircraft	2006	2011-2012	4

$1.6-1.7 b 'E-X' or 'Peace Eye' programme (incl assembly of 3 in South Korea)

(57)	F404	Turbofan	(2006)	2008-2012	(57)

For 57 T-50 trainer and T/A-50 (T-50 LIFT) trainer/combat aircraft produced South Korea; incl production of components and final assembly in South Korea

21	F-15E Strike Eagle	FGA aircraft	2008	2010-2012	21

$2.3 b 'Next Fighter-2' deal; F-15K Slam Eagle version

(60)	F404	Turbofan	2013	2013-2016	(60)

For some 60 FA-50 combat aircraft produced in South Korea; incl production of components and final assembly in South Korea

4	RQ-4A Global Hawk	UAV	2014		

$657 m deal (incl production of components in South Korea); RQ-4B Block-30 version; delivery 2017-2019

6	Mk-41	Naval SAM system	(1999)	2003-2008	6

For 6 Yi Sun-Shin (KDX-2) destroyers produced in South Korea

147	AIM-120C AMRAAM	BVRAAM	2002	2005-2006	(147)

Part of $110 m deal; for F-15K combat aircraft

12	LM-2500	Gas turbine	(2002)	2008-2012	12

For 3 KDX-3 destroyers produced in South Korea

3	Mk-41	Naval SAM system	2002	2008-2012	3

For 3 Daewang (KDX-3) destroyers produced in South Korea

3	Mk-45 127mm	Naval gun	(2002)	2008-2012	3

For 3 KDX-3 destroyers produced in South Korea

9	SPG-62	Fire control radar	(2002)	2008-2012	9

For 3 KDX-3 destroyers produced in South Korea

No.	Designation	Description	Year of order	Year(s) of delivery	No. delivered
3	SPS-67	Sea search radar	(2002)	2008-2012	3

For 3 KDX-3 destroyers produced in South Korea

No.	Designation	Description	Year of order	Year(s) of delivery	No. delivered
3	SPY-1D	Air search radar	(2002)	2008-2012	3

For 3 KDX-3 destroyers produced in South Korea

No.	Designation	Description	Year of order	Year(s) of delivery	No. delivered
3	SQS-53	ASW sonar	(2002)	2008-2012	3

For 3 KDX-3 destroyers produced in South Korea; SQS-53C version

No.	Designation	Description	Year of order	Year(s) of delivery	No. delivered
(40)	Tiger Eyes	Aircraft EO system	2002	2005-2008	(40)

$164 m deal; for F-15K combat aircraft

No.	Designation	Description	Year of order	Year(s) of delivery	No. delivered
(47)	AGM-84H SLAM-ER	ASM	(2003)	2006-2008	(47)

$70 m deal; for F-15K combat aircraft

No.	Designation	Description	Year of order	Year(s) of delivery	No. delivered
27	F404	Turbofan	(2003)	2006-2008	(27)

$80 m deal; F-404-GE-102 version for 25 T-50 trainer aircraft produced in South Korea (including 2 spare engines)

No.	Designation	Description	Year of order	Year(s) of delivery	No. delivered
(14)	JDAM	Guided bomb	2003	2006	(14)
105	AIM-9X Sidewinder	SRAAM	2004	2006-2007	(105)

Part of $110 m deal; for F-15K combat aircraft

No.	Designation	Description	Year of order	Year(s) of delivery	No. delivered
(130)	RIM-116A RAM	SAM	(2004)	2007-2011	(130)

For KDX-3 destroyers and Dodko (LPX) AALS

No.	Designation	Description	Year of order	Year(s) of delivery	No. delivered
(159)	Standard Missile-2MR	SAM	(2004)	2006-2008	(159)

SM-2 Block-3A version; for KDX-2 destroyers

No.	Designation	Description	Year of order	Year(s) of delivery	No. delivered
36	LM-500	Gas turbine	(2005)	2008-2015	(36)

For 18 Gumdoksuri (PKX or PKG-A) FAC produced in South Korea

No.	Designation	Description	Year of order	Year(s) of delivery	No. delivered
8	P-3CUP Orion	ASW aircraft	2005	2010	8

$493-550 m deal; second-hand P-3B rebuilt to P-3CK (P-3CUP); 1 more for spares only

No.	Designation	Description	Year of order	Year(s) of delivery	No. delivered
(22)	APG-67	Combat ac radar	(2006)	2011-2012	(22)

AN/APG-67(V)4 version; for 22 T/A-50 (T-50 LIFT) trainer/combat aircraft produced in South Korea

No.	Designation	Description	Year of order	Year(s) of delivery	No. delivered
26	RGM-84L Harpoon-2	Anti-ship MI/SSM	2006	2007-2008	(26)

$38 m deal; incl 20 AGM-84 and 6 UGM-84 version

No.	Designation	Description	Year of order	Year(s) of delivery	No. delivered
(30)	RIM-116A RAM	SAM	2006	2007	30

$17.4 m deal; RIM-116A Block-1/HAS version

No.	Designation	Description	Year of order	Year(s) of delivery	No. delivered
48	Standard Missile-2MR	SAM	2006	2008	(48)

$111 m deal; SM-2 Block-3B version; for KDX-3 destroyers

No.	Designation	Description	Year of order	Year(s) of delivery	No. delivered
125	AIM-120C AMRAAM	BVRAAM	(2008)	2011-2015	(125)

AIM-120C-7 version

No.	Designation	Description	Year of order	Year(s) of delivery	No. delivered
102	AIM-9X Sidewinder	SRAAM	(2008)	2010-2011	(102)

Part of $55 m deal; for F-15K combat aircraft

No.	Designation	Description	Year of order	Year(s) of delivery	No. delivered
(280)	JDAM	Guided bomb	(2008)	2010-2011	(280)

Part of $200 m deal

No.	Designation	Description	Year of order	Year(s) of delivery	No. delivered
64	MIM-104C PAC-2	SAM	2008	2010-2011	(64)

South Korean PAC-2 missiles rebuilt to GEM-T version

No.	Designation	Description	Year of order	Year(s) of delivery	No. delivered
59	RGM-84L Harpoon-2	Anti-ship MI/SSM	2008	2011	(59)

AGM-84L version

No.	Designation	Description	Year of order	Year(s) of delivery	No. delivered
(210)	Standard Missile-2MR	SAM	2008	2009-2015	(210)

$372 m deal; SM-2 Block-3A and SM-2 Block-3B version; for KDX-3 destroyers

No.	Designation	Description	Year of order	Year(s) of delivery	No. delivered
(40)	AAQ-33 Sniper	Aircraft EO system	(2009)	2010-2013	(40)

For F-15K combat aircraft

No.	Designation	Description	Year of order	Year(s) of delivery	No. delivered
35	AGM-65 Maverick	ASM	2009	2011	(35)

AGM-65G version

No.	Designation	Description	Year of order	Year(s) of delivery	No. delivered
(12)	LM-2500	Gas turbine	(2009)	2013-2016	12

For 6 Incheon (FFX) frigates produced in South Korea

No.	Designation	Description	Year of order	Year(s) of delivery	No. delivered
(6)	Mk-45 127mm	Naval gun	(2009)	2013-2016	6

For 6 Incheon (FFX) frigates produced in South Korea

No.	Designation	Description	Year of order	Year(s) of delivery	No. delivered
(88)	AIM-9L/M Sidewinder	SRAAM	(2010)	2012	(88)

AIM-9L/I-1 version; from FRG production line

No.	Designation	Description	Year of order	Year(s) of delivery	No. delivered
4	C-130J-30 Hercules	Transport aircraft	2010	2014	4
10	MaxxPro	APC	(2010)	2011	(10)

MaxxPro Dash FXM version

No.	Designation	Description	Year of order	Year(s) of delivery	No. delivered
(62)	Standard Missile-2MR	SAM	2010	2012	(62)

$67 m deal; SM-2 Block-3A and SM-2 Block-3B versions; for KDX-3 destroyers

No.	Designation	Description	Year of order	Year(s) of delivery	No. delivered
(150)	GBU-28	Guided bomb	2011	2013	(150)

KWR80 b ($71 m) deal

No.	Designation	Description	Year of order	Year(s) of delivery	No. delivered
6	Mk-15 Phalanx	CIWS	2011	2013-2016	6

Phalanx Block-1B version for 6 Incheon (FFX) frigates produced in South Korea

150	Paveway	Guided bomb	2011	2013	(150)
$71 m deal; GBU-28 Paveway-3 version					
(107)	Paveway	Guided bomb	(2011)	2011	107
$39 m deal; GBU-24 Paveway-3 version					
19	Standard Missile-2MR	SAM	2011	2015	(19)
SM-2 Block-3B version					
(55)	AIM-9X Sidewinder	SRAAM	2012	2012-2013	(55)
246	JDAM	Guided bomb	2012	2013	(246)
(16)	T-800	Turboshaft	(2012)	2016	(16)
For 8 AW-159 helicopters from UK					
(50)	AAQ-33 Sniper	Aircraft EO system	2013	2015-2016	(35)
For F-16C and F-15K combat aircraft; delivery 2015-2017					
288	AGM-114K HELLFIRE	Anti-tank missile	2013	2016	(100)
AGM-114R1 version for AH-64E combat helicopters					
36	AH-64D Apache	Combat helicopter	2013	2016	(14)
$1.6 b 'AH-X' programme; AH-64E version; delivery 2016-2017					
(76)	AIM-9X Sidewinder	SRAAM	(2013)	2016	(40)
6	APG-78 Longbow	Combat heli radar	2013		
For 6 AH-64E combat helicopters					
14	CH-47D Chinook	Transport helicopter	(2013)	2014	14
Second-hand; $151 m deal					
210	JDAM	Guided bomb	2013	2014	(210)
5	T55-L	Turboshaft	(2013)	2014	(5)
Second-hand; T55-GA-714 version; spares for CH-47D helicopters					
2	T-700	Turboshaft	2013	2016	(2)
Spares for AH-64E combat helicopters					
(100)	AGM-65 Maverick	ASM	2014	2015-2016	(100)
$31 m deal					
(274)	AIM-120C AMRAAM	BVRAAM	(2014)	2016	(100)
AIM-120C-7 version					
361	CBU-97 SFW	Guided bomb	2014	2016	(361)
$190 m deal; CBU-105 version					
40	F-35A JSF	FGA aircraft	2014		
KRW7.3 tr ($7 b) 'FX-3' programme (offsets incl technology transfer); delivery from 2018					
(112)	MIM-104C PAC-2	SAM	2014	2016	(50)
$160 m deal; South Korean PAC-2 missiles rebuilt to GEM-T version					
9	Mk-15 Phalanx	CIWS	2014		
$123 m deal; Phalanx Block-1B version for Incheon (FFX) frigates and AOE-2 support ships produced in South Korea					
(62)	AIM-9X Sidewinder	SRAAM	(2015)		
134	APG-83 SABR	Combat ac radar	(2015)		
For modernization of 134 F-16 combat aircraft; delivery from 2018					
38	C32	Diesel engine	(2015)		
For 19 PKX-B FAC produced in South Korea for delivery 2017-2019					
63	FIM-92 Stinger	Portable SAM	2015		
Part of $35 m deal; for AH-64E combat helicopters					
38	LM-500	Gas turbine	(2015)		
For 19 PKX-B FAC produced in South Korea for delivery 2017-2019					
(136)	MIM-104F PAC-3	ABM	2015		
$769 m deal					
8	Patriot PAC-3	SAM/ABM system	(2015)		
South Korean Patriot PAC-2 SAM system rebuilt to Patriot PAC-3 SAM/ABM system					
(240)	F414	Turbofan	(2016)		
For KFX combat aircraft produced in South Korea					
3	SPY-1D	Air search radar	2016		
For 3 KDX-3 destroyers produced in South Korea					

Russia

Images/pixabay.com/Russian flag/Su-35 combat aircraft/parachuting free fall/honour guard

The Russian armed forces have one of the largest militaries in the world. Its main adversaries are the USA and its allies, hence it keeps a strong military to deal with these threats. Russia has 831,000 personnel, with 2,000,000 reserves. Its defence budget is $46.6 billion.

By 2017, Russia had 50,000 personnel working on strategic missiles (Strategic Rocket Force - ICBM sites and SLBM). The Russian army numbers 270,000 with large reserves. It has 2950 MBT (17,500 in store) and 14,132 AIFV/APCs (14,500 in store). The navy has 150,000 personnel and 62 submarines and 33 principal surface warships (including 1 aircraft carrier, 5 cruisers, 15 destroyers and 12 frigates).

The Russian air force has 165,000 personnel with 2095 combat aircraft (strike and heavy bombers).[64] It has the ability to project powers beyond its immediate area. It has continued to develop and purchase sophisticated state of the art weapons. The table below shows the weapons procured from the period 2006 – 2016.

Russia's weapon procurement

Source: SIPRI Arms Transfers Database[65]

Supplier/ recipient (R)	No. ordered	No. designation	Weapon description	Year(s) Weapon of order	Year delivery	of delivered
Czech Republic						
R: Russia	4	L-410 Turbolet	Light transport ac	(2010)	2011	4
	3	L-410 Turbolet	Light transport ac	2011	2012	(3)
	4	L-410 Turbolet	Light transport ac	2012	2013-2014	(4)
L-410NG version; for training						
France						
R: Russia	3	AS-350/AS-550 Fennec	Light helicopter	2012	2013	3
AS-350B version; probably for evaluation						
	2	AS-355/AS-555 Fennec	Light helicopter	2012	2013	2
AS-355N3 version; probably for evaluation						
Germany (FRG)						
R: Russia	(2)	MTU-4000	Diesel engine	(2001)	2006	2
For 1 Scorpion (Project-12300) FAC produced in Russia						
Israel						
R: Russia	(10)	Searcher	UAV	2010	2013-2014	(10)
Searcher-2 version; assembled/produced in Russia; Russian designation Forpost						
	8	I-View-150	UAV	2009	2009-2010	(8)
$37 m deal (part of $50-53 m deal)						
	2	Searcher	UAV	2009	2009-2010	(2)
$12 m deal (part of $53 m deal); Searcher-2 version						
Italy						
R: Russia	(358)	LMV	APV	2011	2012-2014	(358)
Assembled from kits in Russia; Russian designation Rys						

[64] The Military Balance, 01/2017, Volume 117, Issue 1

[65] SIPRI Arms Transfers Database - http://armstrade.sipri.org/armstrade/page/trade_register.php

Turkey

R: Russia	1	Alican Deval	Cargo ship	2015	2015	1

Second-hand; bought for transport of military equipment to Syria; Russian designation Dvinitsa-50

	1	Dadali	Cargo Ship	2015	2015	1

Second-hand; bought for transport of military equipment to Syria; Russian designation Vologda-50

Ukraine

R: Russia	(218)	AI-222	Turbofan	2006	2009-2016	(164)

For 109 Yak-130 trainer/combat aircraft produced in Russia 2009-2018 (but engines probably all delivered to Russian producer of aircraft before Ukraine stopped exports to Russia in 2014 or produced in Russia from 2015)

	19	An-140	Transport aircraft	2011	2012-2016	(17)

An-140-100 version

	15	An-148	Transport aircraft	2013	2013-2016	(11)

RUB18 b deal; An-148-100E version; delivery 2013-2017; status of production uncertain after Ukrainian 2014 ban on military exports to Russia

	(4)	DT-59	Gas turbine	(2005)		

For 2 Project-22350 (Gorshkov) frigates produced in Russia (but engines all delivered to Russian producer of aircraft before Ukraine stopped exports to Russia in 2014 and more frigates ordered but cancelled due Ukrainian export ban)

	100	Kh-59M/AS-18 Kazoo	ASM	(2006)	2007	100

Status uncertain; possibly more delivered before 2007

	(6)	DS-71	Gas turbine	(2010)	2016	(2)

For 3 Project-11356 (Grigorovich) frigates produced in Russia (but engines all delivered to Russian producer of aircraft before Ukraine stopped exports to Russia in 2014 and more frigates ordered but cancelled due Ukrainian export ban)

	(6)	DT-59	Gas turbine	(2010)	2015	(2)

For 3 Project-11356 (Grigorovich) frigates produced in Russia (but engines all delivered to Russian producer of aircraft before Ukraine stopped exports to Russia in 2014 and more frigates ordered but cancelled due Ukrainian export ban)

Unknown supplier(s)

R: Russia	(1)	Georgiy Agafonov	Cargo ship	2015	2015	(1)

Second-hand; Ukrainian merchant ship sold to Turkish company for scrap or civilian use, resold to UK company and bought by Russian navy via Mongolian and/or Russian company for transport of military equipment to Syria; Russian designation Kazan-60

Philippines

Images/pixabay.com/Philippines flag

The Philippines armed forces are geared towards protecting its territorial integrity and its areas of interest. It has 125,000 personnel with 131,000 reserves. It's defence budget amounts to $2,54 billion. By 2017, Philippines army numbers 86,000 with 100,000 reserves. It has 7 Light Tanks and 491 AIFV/APCs. The navy has 24,000 personnel and 1 principal surface warship. The Philippines air force has 15,000 personnel with 24 combat aircraft.[66] The table below shows the weapons procured from the period 2006 – 2016.

Philippine's weapon procurement

Source: SIPRI Arms Transfers Database[67]

---

[66] The Military Balance, 01/2017, Volume 117, Issue 1

Supplier/ recipient (R)	No. ordered	Weapon designation	Weapon description	Year(s) of order	Year of delivery	No. delivered
Australia						
R: Philippines	2	Balikpapan	Landing craft	2015	2015	2
Second-hand; aid						
	3	Balikpapan	Landing craft	(2015)	2016	3
Second-hand; PHP270 m deal						
Belgium						
R: Philippines	24	M-113	APC	2014	2015	24
Second-hand but modernized before delivery; part of PNP882 m ($20 m) deal; incl 4 modified to IFV and 14 modified to AFSV (with second-hand Philippine turret)						
Canada						
R: Philippines	(6)	PW100	Turboprop/turboshaft	2014	2015	(6)
For 3 C-295 transport aircraft from Spain						
France						
R: Philippines	2	FLASH	ASW sonar	2016		
For 2 AW-159 ASW helicopters from UK						
Germany (FRG)						
R: Philippines	5	Bell-205/UH-1D	Helicopter	(2013)	2013	5
Second-hand						
Indonesia						
R: Philippines	2	C-212	Transport aircraft	2014		
PHP814 m ($18 m) deal; NC-212i version; delivery 2017						
	2	LPD-122m	AALS	2014	2016	1
PHP3.9 b ($90 m) 'SSV' programme; Philippine designation Tarlac; delivery 2016-2017						
Israel						
R: Philippines	12	EL/M-2032	Combat ac radar	(2014)	2015-2016	(4)
For 12 FA-50 combat aircraft from South Korea						
	4	UT-25/UT-30	IFV turret	2014	2015	(4)
UT-25 version for 4 second-hand M-113A2 APC (from Belgium) modified to IFV						
	3	EL/M-2288 AD-STAR	Air search radar	2015		
$56 m deal; delivery 2017						
		Spike-ER	Anti-tank missile	2016		
For MPAC patrol craft						
		Spike-NLOS	SSM/ASM	2016		
For AW159 helicopters						
Italy						
R: Philippines	18	SF-260	Trainer aircraft	2008	2010-2011	18
$13 m deal (incl production of components and assembly in Philippines); SF-260F/PAF version						
	3	A-109K	Light helicopter	2012	2013	3
PHP1.3 b ($33 m) deal; AW109P version						
	8	A-109K	Light helicopter	2013	2015	8
$77 m deal; armed AW109P version						
	2	A-109K	Light helicopter	2014	2015	2
AW109P version						
Japan						
R: Philippines	5	King Air	Light transport ac	2016		
Second-hand; lease; King Air-90 (TC-90A) version; delivery 2017						
Netherlands						
R: Philippines	4	AIFV-APC	APC	2015	2015	4
Second-hand; EUR0.31m deal (incl 1 more delivered for spare parts only; part of PNP882 m ($20 m) deal ordered and						

[67] SIPRI Arms Transfers Database - http://armstrade.sipri.org/armstrade/page/trade_register.php

delivered via Belgian company; modernized in Belgium before delivery); YPR-806 ARV version

Poland

	No.	Weapon designation	Weapon description	Year of order	Year of delivery	No. delivered
R: Philippines	8	W-3 Sokol	Helicopter	2011	2012-2013	8

PHP2.8 b ($64 m) deal

South Korea

	No.	Weapon designation	Weapon description	Year of order	Year of delivery	No. delivered
R: Philippines	2	Sea Dolphin	Patrol craft	(2004)	2006	2

Second-hand

	(15)	Cessna-172/T-41	Trainer/light ac	2007	2009	15

Second-hand; T-41D version

	12	FA-50	FGA aircraft	2014	2015-2016	4

Possibly PHP18-18.9 b ($360-430 m) deal; delivery 2015-2017

	1	LCU-1610	Landing craft	2014	2016	1

Second-hand; aid

	1	Po Hang	Corvette	(2014)		

Second-hand; aid

	8	AAV-7A1	APC	2016		

PHP2.4 b ($53 m) deal; delivery by 2018

	2	HHI-2600	Frigate	2016		

PHP15.7 b ($311 m) 'Deep Water Patrol Vessel' programme; delivery from 2020

Spain

	No.	Weapon designation	Weapon description	Year of order	Year of delivery	No. delivered
R: Philippines	3	C-295	Transport aircraft	2014	2015-2016	3

PHP5.3 b ($120 m) deal

Turkey

	No.	Weapon designation	Weapon description	Year of order	Year of delivery	No. delivered
R: Philippines	6	AIFV-APC	APC	2007	2010	6

ACV-300 version

United Kingdom

	No.	Weapon designation	Weapon description	Year of order	Year of delivery	No. delivered
R: Philippines	1	F-27 Friendship	Transport aircraft	2005	2007	1

Second-hand

	2	AW-159 Wildcat	ASW helicopter	2016		

PHP5.4 b deal; delivery by 2018

United States

	No.	Weapon designation	Weapon description	Year of order	Year of delivery	No. delivered
R: Philippines	20	Bell-205/UH-1H	Helicopter	2003	2007-2008	(20)

Second-hand; part of $30 m aid (10 more delivered for spare parts)

	(6)	Bell-205/UH-1H	Helicopter	2003	2006-2007	(6)

Second-hand but modernized before delivery; $8.2 m deal

	48	M-113	APC	(2003)	2006	(48)

Second-hand; aid

	12	6BT	Diesel engine	(2006)	2007	12

6CTA version; for modernization of 12 V-150 APC

	6	6V-53	Diesel engine	2007	2009	6

For 6 AIFV-APC (ACV-300) APC from Turkey; 6V-53T version

	5	Bell-205/UH-1H	Helicopter	(2009)	2011	5

Second-hand; possibly modernized before delivery

	2	Hunter	UAV	(2009)	2009	2

Second-hand

	1	Hamilton	OPV	2011	2011	1

Second-hand; $27 m deal (aid but overhaul and delivery paid by Philippines); Philippine designation Del Pilar

	(22)	JDAM	Guided bomb	2011	2011	(22)
	1	TPS-79 MMSR	Air search radar	(2011)	2012	(1)

Designation uncertain (reported as 'coastal radar')

	1	Hamilton	OPV	2012	2013	1

Second-hand; $16 m deal (aid but overhaul and delivery paid by Philippines); Philippine designation Del Pilar

	114	M-113	APC	2012	2015	114

Second-hand; aid; M-113A2 version

	(7)	Bell-205/UH-1H	Helicopter	2013	2014	(7)

Second-hand but modernized before delivery; originally PHP1.25 b deal for 21 but 14 cancelled due to delivery delays

	(25)	HMMWV Up-Armoured	APV	2013	2013	(25)

Second-hand; M-1114 version; aid

(6)	Bell-412	Helicopter	2014	2015	(6)

Part of $105 m deal; Bell-412EP version; from Canadian production line; 2 more delivered for government VIP transport

2	C-130H Hercules	Transport aircraft	(2014)	2016	2

Second-hand; $56 m deal (incl $20 m aid); C-130T version

(12)	F404	Turbofan	(2014)	2015-2016	(4)

For 12 FA-50 combat aircraft from South Korea

2	T56	Turboprop	(2014)	2016	(2)

Second-hand; spares for C-130 transport aircraft

1	Hamilton	OPV	(2015)	2016	1

Second-hand; aid; Philippine designation Del Pilar

(2)	Cessna-208 Caravan	Light transport ac	2016	

Cessna-208B surveillance version; delivery probably 2017

4	T-800	Turboshaft	2016	

For 2 AW-159 ASW helicopters from UK

Indonesia

Images/pixabay.com/Indonesian flag

The Indonesian armed forces are geared towards protecting its territorial integrity and its areas of interest. It has 395,500 personnel with 131,000 reserves. It's defence budget amounts to $2,54 billion. By 2017, Philippines army numbers 300,400 with 400,000 reserves. It has 49 MBT and 415 Light Tanks and 815 AIFV/APCs. The navy has 65,000 personnel 2 submarines and 12 principal surface warship (frigates). The Indonesian air force has 30,100 personnel with 111 combat aircraft.[68] The table below shows the weapons procured from the period 2006 – 2016.

Indonesia's weapon procurement

Source: SIPRI Arms Transfers Database[69]

Supplier/ recipient (R)	No. ordered	Weapon designation	description	Year(s) Weapon of order	Year delivery	of delivered
Australia						
R: Indonesia	50	Bushmaster	APC	(2016)		
Indonesian designation Sanca; selected but probably not yet ordered by end-2016						
	3	Bushmaster	APC	2013	2014	3
	4	C-130H Hercules	Transport aircraft	2013	2013-2015	(4)
Second-hand but modernized for AUD63 m before delivery; aid						
	5	C-130H Hercules	Transport aircraft	(2015)	2016	(1)
Second-hand; delivery 2017						
Belgium						
R: Indonesia	50	CM-90 90mm	Tank turret	2016	2016	(10)
For 50 Badak DFV armoured fire support vehicles produced in Indonesia						
	(22)	CM-90 90mm	Tank turret	(2008)	2013	(22)
For Black Fox IFV from South Korea; CSE-90 version						

---

[68] The Military Balance, 01/2017, Volume 117, Issue 1

[69] SIPRI Arms Transfers Database - http://armstrade.sipri.org/armstrade/page/trade_register.php

150	M-113	APC	2014	2014-2016	(95)

Second-hand; incl ARV version

20	M-109A1 155mm	Self-propelled gun	2016		

Second-hand; M-109A4 version

Brazil

R: Indonesia

8	EMB-314 Super Tucano	Trainer/combat ac	2011	2012-2014	8
(36)	ASTROS-2	Self-propelled MRL	2012	2014-2015	(36)

$403 m deal; ASTROS-2 Mk-6 version

8	EMB-314 Super Tucano	Trainer/combat ac	2012	2015-2016	8

Brunei

R: Indonesia

2	Waspada	FAC	2010	2011	2

Second-hand; aid; for training

Canada

R: Indonesia

(5)	PT6	Turboprop/turboshaft	2005	2007-2008	(5)

For 5 KT-1 trainer aircraft from South Korea; PT-6A-62A version

(8)	PT6	Turboprop/turboshaft	(2005)	2011-2012	(8)

For 8 KT-1 trainer aircraft from South Korea; PT-6A-62A version

(8)	PT6	Turboprop/turboshaft	2011	2012-2014	(8)

For 8 EMB-314 trainer/combat aircraft from Brazil

(8)	PT6	Turboprop/turboshaft	2012	2015-2016	(8)

For 8 EMB-314 trainer/combat aircraft from Brazil

(18)	PW100	Turboprop/turboshaft	2012	2012-2015	(18)

PW127 version for 9 C-295 transport aircraft from Spain

China

R: Indonesia

(3)	C-802/CSS-N-8	Anti-ship missile	2005	2008	(3)

Part of $11.2 m deal; for PB-57 (Todak) FAC; for evaluation

(130)	QW-3	Portable SAM	(2006)	2006-2007	(130)

Incl for Indonesian UN peacekeeping force in Lebanon

(200)	QW-3	Portable SAM	2008	2012-2013	(200)

For TD-2000B AD system

(2)	SR-74	Air search radar	(2008)	2012-2013	(2)

For use with TD-2000B AD systems

(8)	TD-2000B	AD system	2008	2012-2013	(8)

Part of $35 m deal

(15)	QW-3	Portable SAM	2009	2010	(15)
(3)	TH-5711 Smart Hunter	Air search radar	2009	2011	(3)

For use with QW-3 SAM

(24)	Type-360 Seagull	Air search radar	(2009)	2011-2014	(8)
(250)	C-705	Anti-ship missile	(2011)	2014-2016	(56)

For KCR-40 and KCR-60 FAC; including assembly from kits or production in Indonesia from 2017/2018

(50)	C-802/CSS-N-8	Anti-ship missile	2011	2012-2016	(50)

For PB-57 (Todak) FAC and Van Speyk (Ahmad Yani) frigates

(24)	NG-18 30mm	Naval gun	(2013)	2013-2014	(8)

For 24 KCR-40 FAC produced in Indonesia

1	Type-825 30mm	Naval gun/CIWS	(2014)	2015	1

For modernization of 1 Pattimura (Parchim) corvette

4	GDF 35mm	AA gun	2015	2016	4

Type-90 version

1	Skyguard	Fire control radar	2015	2016	1

AF-902 version; for use with GDF (Type-90) 35mm anti-aircraft guns

4	Type-90 122mm	Self-propelled MRL	2015	2016	4

Type-90B version

1	Type-825 30mm	Naval gun/CIWS	2016		

For modernization of 1 Pattimura (Parchim) corvette; delivery 2017

Czech Republic

R: Indonesia

3	RM-70 122mm	Self-propelled MRL	(2007)	2008	3

Second-hand
| | (36) | RM-70 122mm | Self-propelled MRL | 2014 | 2016 | 8 |

Second-hand; modernized to RM-70 Vampir version before delivery

Denmark
| R: Indonesia | 8 | B&W-8L | Diesel engine | 2004 | 2007-2011 | 8 |

For 4 LPD-122m landing ships from South Korea; possibly from South Korean production line
| | 1 | Scanter-4100 | Air/sea search radar | 2013 | 2015 | (1) |

For modernization of 1 Fatahillah frigate

France
| R: Indonesia | (10) | AS-532 Cougar/AS-332 | Transport helicopter | 1997 | 2001-2015 | (8) |

NAS-332 version; incl some for CSAR
| | (100) | Sherpa | APV | 2011 | 2011-2015 | (100) |

Indonesian designation Elang
| | (9) | Ocean Master | MP aircraft radar | 1996 | 2000-2007 | (9) |

For 6 C-212MP (NC-212MP) MP aircraft from Spain and 3 Bo-105 (NBo-105) helicopters from FRG
| | 3 | Ocean Master | MP aircraft radar | 2001 | 2008 | (3) |

$50 m deal; for 3 CN-235MPA aircraft produced in Indonesia
| | 6 | 20PA6 | Diesel engine | 2004 | 2006-2007 | 6 |

For 2 SIGMA-90 frigates from Netherlands and modernization of 1 Yani (Van Speijk) frigate
| | 1 | Master | Air search radar | 2004 | 2006 | (1) |

Master-T version
| | (80) | Mistral | Portable SAM | 2004 | 2007 | (80) |

For SIGMA-90 frigates
| | (30) | MM-40 Exocet | Anti-ship missile | (2004) | 2010 | (30) |

MM-40 Block-2 version; for SIGMA-90 frigates
| | 2 | TSM-2633 Spherion-B | ASW sonar | 2004 | 2007 | 2 |

Kingklip version for 2 SIGMA-90 frigates from Netherlands
| | 4 | 20PA6 | Diesel engine | 2005 | 2008-2009 | 4 |

For 2 SIGMA-90 frigates from Netherlands
| | (80) | Mistral | Portable SAM | 2005 | 2008-2009 | (80) |

For SIGMA-90 frigates
| | 2 | TSM-2633 Spherion-B | ASW sonar | 2005 | 2008-2009 | 2 |

Kingklip version for 2 SIGMA-90 frigates from Netherlands
| | 150 | MIDR | Diesel engine | 2006 | 2008-2012 | (150) |

For Anao (APS-3 or Panser 6x6) APC produced in Indonesia
| | (32) | VAB-VTT | APC | 2006 | 2007 | (32) |

EUR24 m deal; possibly second-hand but modernized; incl 6 ambulance and 2 CP version; for use with Indonesian UN troops in Lebanon
| | (2) | EC-120 Colibri | Light helicopter | (2008) | 2009 | (2) |

For training
| | 3 | Master | Air search radar | 2008 | 2011-2012 | 3 |

Master-T version
| | (1) | Ocean Master | MP aircraft radar | 2009 | 2013 | 1 |

For 1 CN-235MPA MP aircraft produced in Indonesia
| | 12 | MIDR | Diesel engine | (2010) | 2013 | (12) |

For Anao (APS-3 or Panser 6x6) APC produced in Indonesia
| | 6 | AS-350/AS-550 Fennec | Light helicopter | (2012) | 2014 | (1) |

Armed AS-550 version
| | 6 | AS-355/AS-555 Fennec | Light helicopter | 2012 | 2016 | (3) |

Armed AS-555 version
| | 37 | CAESAR 155mm | Self-propelled gun | 2012 | 2014-2015 | (37) |
| | 6 | EC725 Super Cougar | Transport helicopter | 2012 | 2016 | 2 |

Armed combat SAR version; delivery 2016-2017
| | (136) | Mistral | Portable SAM | (2012) | 2013-2016 | (136) |

For use with ATLAS launchers on Komodo APC produced in Indonesia
| | 2 | TSM-2633 Spherion-B | ASW sonar | 2013 | | |

Kingklip version for 2 SIGMA-105 frigates from Netherlands
| | 11 | AS565S Panther | ASW helicopter | 2014 | | |

AS565MBe version; assembled in Indonesia; delivery probably 2017-2018/2019

No.	Designation	Description	Year of order	Year of delivery	No. delivered
(5)	Ground Master-200	Air search radar	2014	2016	(2)

Part of Controlmaster-200 command system for Forceshield SAM system from UK

| (40) | MICA | BVRAAM | 2016 | | |

VL-MICA SAM version for SIGMA-10514 frigates

| (50) | MIDR | Diesel engine | (2016) | 2016 | (10) |

For 50 Badak DFV armoured fire support vehicles produced in Indonesia

| (30) | MM-40 Exocet | Anti-ship missile | 2016 | | |

For SIGMA-10514 frigates

| 2 | VL-MICA-M | Naval SAM system | 2016 | | |

For 2 SIGMA-10514 frigates from Netherlands

Germany (FRG)

R: Indonesia

| (57) | Bo-105 | Light helicopter | 1976 | 1977-2011 | (57) |

Indonesian designation NBO-105CB/CBS; incl for police

| (72) | D2862 | Diesel engine | (2009) | 2011-2014 | (24) |

For 16 KCR-40 FAC produced in Indonesia

| 18 | G-120TP | Trainer aircraft | 2011 | 2013-2014 | (18) |

$72 m deal

| 2 | BPz-2 | ARV | 2012 | 2015 | (2) |

Second-hand; part of EUR216 m deal

| 3 | BrPz-1 Biber | ABL | 2012 | 2015-2016 | 3 |

Second-hand Leopard-2 tank modified to Buffel ARV

| 61 | Leopard-2A4 | Tank | 2012 | 2016 | 40 |

Second-hand but modernized to Leopard-2RI before delivery; delivery 2016-2017

| 42 | Leopard-2A4 | Tank | 2012 | 2013-2015 | 42 |

Second-hand; part of EUR216 m deal

| (42) | Marder-1A3 | IFV | 2012 | 2013-2015 | (42) |

Second-hand (possibly modernized before delivery; 8 more delivered for spare parts only); part of EUR216 m deal

| 3 | PiPz-1 | AEV | 2012 | 2016 | 3 |

Second-hand; part of EUR216 m deal

| 12 | EC135 | Light helicopter | (2013) | | |

EC-135 version

| (20) | TP400-D6 | Turboprop | (2016) | | |

For 5 A400M transport aircraft from Spain

Israel

R: Indonesia

| 4 | Searcher | UAV | 2006 | 2012 | (4) |

Italy

R: Indonesia

| (40) | A244 324mm | ASW torpedo | (2004) | 2007 | (40) |

For SIGMA-90 frigates

| 2 | Super Rapid 76mm | Naval gun | 2004 | 2007 | 2 |

For 2 SIGMA-90 frigates from Netherlands

| 2 | Super Rapid 76mm | Naval gun | 2005 | 2008-2009 | 2 |

For 2 SIGMA-90 frigates from Netherlands

| (12) | A244 324mm | ASW torpedo | 2006 | 2008-2009 | (12) |

For SIGMA-90 frigates

| 2 | Super Rapid 76mm | Naval gun | (2012) | | |

For 2 SIGMA-105 frigates from Netherlands

| 3 | Super Rapid 76mm | Naval gun | 2013 | 2014 | 3 |

Netherlands

R: Indonesia

| 1 | SIGMA-105 | Frigate | 2012 | | |

$220 m deal (incl production of components and assembly in Indonesia); part of 'PKR' programme; SIGMA-10514 version; delivery 2017

| 1 | SIGMA-105 | Frigate | 2013 | | |

Incl production of components and assembly in Indonesia; part of 'PKR' programme; SIGMA-10514 version; delivery 2017

| 2 | SIGMA-90 | Frigate | 2004 | 2007 | 2 |

$340 m deal (payment spread over 3 years)

| 2 | SIGMA-90 | Frigate | 2005 | 2008-2009 | 2 |
| 3 | Scout | Sea search radar | 2013 | 2014 | 3 |

For 3 Brunei (Bung Tomo) frigates from UK

New Zealand

| **R:** Indonesia | (1) | Klewang | FAC | 2014 | | |

Delivery 2017

Poland

| **R:** Indonesia | (74) | Grom-2 | Portable SAM | 2005 | 2007 | 74 |

Part of $35 m deal (incl 15% paid direct + $30 m with Polish loan); for Kobra SAM system

| | 1 | Kobra MMSR | AD system | 2005 | 2007 | 1 |

Part of $35 m deal (incl 15% paid direct + $30 m with Polish loan)

| | (81) | Grom-2 | Portable SAM | 2006 | 2009 | 81 |

Part of $40 m deal; for Kobra SAM system

| | 1 | Kobra MMSR | AD system | 2006 | 2009 | 1 |

Part of $40 m deal

Russia

| **R:** Indonesia | 6 | Mi-8MT/Mi-17 | Transport helicopter | (2005) | 2008 | 6 |

Mi-17V-5 armed version

| | 17 | BMP-3 | IFV | 2008 | 2010 | 17 |

IDR455 m ($40-50m) deal; BMP-3F version

| | 1 | BREM-L | ARV | 2008 | 2010 | 1 |
| | (3) | Mi-24P/Mi-35P | Combat helicopter | (2008) | 2010 | 3 |

Mi-35P version

| | (75) | R-73/AA-11 | SRAAM | (2008) | 2010 | (75) |

For Su-27 and Su-30 combat aircraft

| | (60) | RVV-AE/AA-12 Adder | BVRAAM | (2008) | 2012-2013 | (60) |

For Su-27 and Su-30 combat aircraft

| | 3 | Su-27S/Flanker-B | FGA aircraft | 2008 | 2010 | 3 |

Part of $300-353 m deal; Su-27SKM-2 version

| | 3 | Su-30MK | FGA aircraft | 2008 | 2009 | 3 |

Part of $300-353 m deal; Su-30MK2 version

| | (10) | Kh-29/AS-14 Kedge | ASM | (2009) | 2012 | (10) |
| | (10) | Kh-31A1/AS-17 | Anti-ship missile/ARM | (2009) | 2011-2012 | (10) |

Kh-31P anti-radar version

| | (10) | Kh-59M/AS-18 Kazoo | ASM | (2009) | 2012 | (10) |
| | (10) | Yakhont/SS-N-26 | Anti-ship missile | (2009) | 2011 | (10) |

For modernized Yani (Van Speyk) frigate

| | 6 | Mi-8MT/Mi-17 | Transport helicopter | 2010 | 2011 | 6 |

$56 m deal; Mi-17-V5 armed version

| | 6 | Su-30MK | FGA aircraft | 2012 | 2013 | 6 |

$470 m deal; Su-30MK2 version

| | 37 | BMP-3 | IFV | 2013 | 2014 | 37 |

$114 m deal; BMP-3F version

| | (8) | Su-35 | FGA aircraft | (2016) | | |

Selected but not yet ordered by end-2016

South Korea

| **R:** Indonesia | 4 | LPD-122m | AALS | 2004 | 2007-2011 | 4 |

$150 m deal; incl 2 produced in Indonesia; incl 1 for use as command ship; Indonesian designation Soeharso

| | 22 | Black Fox | IFV | 2009 | 2013-2014 | (22) |

$70 m deal; Tarantula version; including 11 produced in Indonesia

| | (50) | KFX | FGA aircraft | (2010) | | |

Possibly $1.6 b deal (Indonesia financing up to 20% of development cost; including limited Indonesian involvement in development); Indonesian designation IFX; selected but not yet ordered by end-2016; delivery after 2025

| | 3 | Type-209/1200 | Submarine | 2011 | | |

KRW1.3tr ($1.1-1.4 b) deal; incl 1 produced in Indonesia; delivery 2017-2018

| | 8 | KT-1 Woong Bee | Trainer aircraft | (2005) | 2011-2012 | (8) |

KT-1B version

| | 5 | KT-1 Woong Bee | Trainer aircraft | 2005 | 2007-2008 | 5 |

Kt-1B version

| | (10) | LVTP-7 | APC | 2009 | 2009 | (10) |

Second-hand; LVTP-7A1 version; aid

	(54)	KH-178 105mm	Towed gun	(2010)	2011	(54)
Probably second-hand M-101A1 rebuilt to KH-178 or possibly second-hand KH-178						
	(36)	KH-179 155mm	Towed gun	(2011)	2012-2014	36
Probably second-hand						
	16	T-50 Golden Eagle	Trainer/combat ac	2011	2013-2014	16
$400 m deal; T-50i version						
	(80)	Chiron	Portable SAM	2012	2013-2015	(80)

Spain

R: Indonesia	(6)	C-212MP	MP aircraft	1996	2005-2007	(6)
Part of $50 m 'On Top-2' programme; NC-212-200MP version						
	(6)	C-212	Transport aircraft	2009	2013-2016	(6)
NC-212-200 version						
	9	C-295	Transport aircraft	2012	2012-2015	(9)
$325 m deal; Indonesian designation CN-295						
	5	A400M Atlas	Transport aircraft	(2016)		
$2 b deal; selected but not yet ordered end-2016						

Sweden

R: Indonesia	(4)	SAK-70 Mk-2 57mm	Naval gun	(2011)	2014-2015	(3)
SAK-70 Mk-3 version; for 4 KCR-60 FAC produced in Indonesia						
		Skeldar	UAV	2016		
Skeldra V-200 version; delivery 2017						

Switzerland

R: Indonesia	(2)	Fieldguard	Fire control radar	(2012)	2014-2015	(2)
Fieldguard-3 version for use with ASTROS MRL						
	6	Skyshield-35	AA gun system	2012	2014-2015	(6)
$202 m deal						
	2	Skyshield-35	AA gun system	2014	2015	2
Delivery 2015						
	2	GDM-008 35mm	CIWS	2016		
For 2 SIGMA-10514 frigates from Netherlands						

Ukraine

R: Indonesia	2	BTR-4	IFV	2014	2016	2
BTR-4M version						
	(3)	BTR-4K	APC	2014	2016	3
	(2)	R-27/AA-10	BVRAAM	2014	2015	2

United Kingdom

R: Indonesia	(500)	Starstreak	Portable SAM	(2012)	2015-2016	(402)
For Forceshield SAM system						
	3	Brunei	Frigate	2013	2014	3
Originally produced for Brunei but cancelled and sold to Indonesia; Indonesian designation Bung Tomo						
	5	Forceshield	SAM system	2014	2016	(2)
$165 m deal						
	(6)	EH-101-400	Transport helicopter	(2015)		
Status uncertain						

United States

R: Indonesia	(76)	CT7	Turboprop	(1990)	1993-2014	(52)
CT-7-9C3 version for 38 CN-235 transport and CN-235MPA MP aircraft produced in Indonesia						
	16	APG-66	Combat ac radar	1996	1999-2007	(16)
For 16 Hawk-200 combat aircraft from UK; status of last 6 uncertain after US arms embargo during 1999-2006 against Indonesia						
	1	F-5E Tiger-2	FGA aircraft	(1996)	2006	1
Second-hand but modernized in USA; delivery embargoed by USA 1999-2006						
	(12)	TPE-331	Turboprop	1996	2005-2007	(12)
For 6 C-212 MP aircraft from Spain						
	8	Caterpillar-3616	Diesel engine	(2006)	2007-2008	8
For modernization of 4 Yani (Van Speijk) frigates						
	(25)	Bell-412	Helicopter	2010	2012-2014	(25)
Bell-412EP version						

(2)	Cessna-180 Skywagon	Light aircraft	(2010)	2011	2
Cessna-182 version					
4	F100	Turbofan	(2011)	2014-2015	(4)
Second-hand; spares for F-16 combat aircraft					
(16)	F404	Turbofan	2011	2013-2014	(16)
For 16 T-50 trainer/combat aircraft from South Korea					
(4)	APG-78 Longbow	Combat heli radar	(2012)		
For 4 AH-64E combat helicopters					
24	F-16C	FGA aircraft	2012	2014-2016	(14)
Second-hand F-16C Block-25 delivered as aid but modernized before delivery to Block-52 version in $670-750 m deal; incl F-16D version (6 more delivered for spare parts only); delivery 2014-2017					
2	Model-300	Light helicopter	2012	2012	(2)
S-300C version; for training; option on 4 more					
(3)	T-700	Turboshaft	(2012)		
Spares for AH-64E combat helicopters					
2	APS-143(V)	MP aircraft radar	(2013)	2014	2
For 2 CN-235MPA MP aircraft produced in Indonesia					
4	Bonanza	Light aircraft	2013	2013	4
Bonanza G-36 version					
3	Caterpillar-3126	Diesel engine	2013	2014	3
For 3 Bushmaster APC from Australia					
(180)	FGM-148 Javelin	Anti-tank missile	2013	2014-2015	(180)
Javelin Block-1 version					
(140)	AGM-114K HELLFIRE	Anti-tank missile	2014		
AGM-114R-3 version for AH-64E combat helicopters					
8	AH-64D Apache	Combat helicopter	(2014)		
$500 m deal; AH-64E version					
(2)	Baron	Light transport ac.	(2014)	2015	2
G58 Baron version; for training					
4	Bonanza	Light aircraft	2014	2015	4
11	HELRAS	ASW sonar	2014		
For 11 AS565S (AS-565MBe) ASW helicopters from France					

Malaysia

Images/pixabay.com/Malaysian flag/automatic weapon-bullet

The Malaysian armed forces are geared towards protecting its territorial integrity and its areas of interest. It has 109,000 personnel with 51,600 reserves. It's defence budget amounts to $4,22 billion. By 2017, Malaysian army numbers 80,000 with 50,000 reserves. It has 48 MBT and 21 Light Tanks and 848 AIFV/APCs. The navy has 14,000 personnel 2 submarines and 10 principal surface warship (frigates). The Malaysian air force has 15,000 personnel with 67 combat aircraft.[70] The table below shows the weapons procured from the period 2006 – 2016.

Malaysia's weapon procurement

Source: SIPRI Arms Transfers Database[71]

---

[70] The Military Balance, 01/2017, Volume 117, Issue 1

[71] SIPRI Arms Transfers Database - http://armstrade.sipri.org/armstrade/page/trade_register.php

Supplier/ recipient (R)	No. ordered	designation	Weapon description	Year(s) of order	Weapon Year delivery	Year(s) of delivered
Brazil						
R: Malaysia	18	ASTROS-2	Self-propelled MRL	2007	2010	18
$300 m deal						
	3	ASTROS AV-UCF	Fire control radar	2007	2010	3
Brunei						
R: Malaysia	4	S-70/UH-60L	Helicopter	(2014)	2016	4
Second-hand						
Canada						
R: Malaysia	10	PT6	Turboprop/turboshaft	2006	2007	10
For 10 PC-7 Mk-2 trainer aircraft from Switzerland; PT-6A-25C version						
	(5)	PT6	Turboprop/turboshaft	(2013)	2016	5
For 5 PC-7 trainer aircraft from Switzerland						
China						
R: Malaysia	4	LMS-68	OPV	(2016)		
Incl 2 produced in Malaysia; selected but not yet ordered by end-2016						
	64	FN-6	Portable SAM	2008	2009	(64)
Denmark						
R: Malaysia	2	Scanter-6000	Air/sea search radar	2016		
For modernization of 2 Lekiu frigates						
France						
R: Malaysia	6	Gowind-2500	Frigate	2014		
'SGVP-LCS' programme; delivery from 2019						
	1	Scorpene	Submarine	2002	2009	1
Part of EUR1.2 b deal (incl 1 more from Spain; incl over 50% barter); Malaysian designation Abdul Rahman						
	40	SM-39 Exocet	Anti-ship missile	2002	2008-2012	(40)
SM-39 Block-2 version: for Scorpene submarines						
	8	Damocles	Aircraft EO system	2004	2007-2009	(8)
Part of EUR150m deal for avionics for Su-30MKM combat aircraft from Russia						
	(2)	TSM-2022	MCM sonar	(2006)	2007	2
For modernization of 2 Lerici (Mahamiru) MCM ships; TSM-2022 Mk-3 version						
	1	Ground Master-400	Air search radar	2008	2013	1
	8	2R2M 120MM	Mortar	2010	2010	(8)
MYR60 m ($19 m) deal; for 8 ACV-S mortar carriers from Turkey						
	12	EC725 Super Cougar	Transport helicopter	2010	2012-2014	(12)
MYR1.6 b ($500 m) deal; for SAR						
	8	2R2M 120MM	Mortar	(2011)		
For 8 Pars (AV-8) mortar carriers from Turkey						
	6	CAPTAS TAS	ASW sonar	2014		
CAPTAS-2 version for 6 Gowind frigates						
	5	EC-120 Colibri	Light helicopter	2015	2016	(3)
	(1)	Ground Master-200	Air search radar	2015	2016	(1)
For use with Forcefield SAM system						
		MICA	BVRAAM	(2015)		
For 6 Combat Gowind (SGVP-LCS) frigates						
Germany (FRG)						
R: Malaysia	6	MEKO-A100	Frigate	1999	2006-2010	6
MYR6.8 b ($2 b) 'New Generation Patrol Vessel' (NGPV) programme (offsets incl production of at least 30% of components and assembly of 4 in Malaysia; original MYR5.4 b cost increased with MYR1.4 b and delivery delayed due to problems of producer); MEKO-10						
	8	MAN V6	Diesel engine	2002	2009	8
For 2 Scorpene submarines from France and Spain						
	(16)	TP400-D6	Turboprop	2005	2015-2016	(16)
For 4 A400M transport aircraft from Spain						

	2	TRML-3D	Air/sea search radar	2005	2008	(2)

EUR18-20 m deal

	2	DSQS-24	ASW sonar	(2009)	2013-2014	2
	(257)	BFM-2015	Diesel engine	2010	2014-2016	(80)

For 257 Pars APC and IFV from Turkey

Indonesia

R: Malaysia	2	CN-235	Transport aircraft	2002	2005-2006	(2)

$34 m deal; possibly second-hand; incl for VIP transport

Italy

R: Malaysia	11	A-109K	Light helicopter	2003	2005-2006	(11)

$70-75 m deal (offsets incl assembly of some in Malaysia and technology transfer); A-109LOH version armed with 20mm gun and/or rockets

	6	Super Rapid 76mm	Naval gun	(2000)	2006-2010	(6)

For 6 MEKO-A100 (Kedah) frigates from FRG

	6	TMX	Fire control radar	(2000)	2006-2010	(6)

For 6 MEKO-A100 (Kedah) frigates from FRG

	(30)	Black Shark	AS/ASW torpedo	2002	2009	(30)

For Scorpene submarines

	8	MB-339C	Trainer/combat ac	2006	2009	8

EUR89 m deal; MB-339CM version

	12	TMX	Fire control radar	(2014)		

For 6 Gowind frigates from France

Netherlands

R: Malaysia	6	SMART	Air search radar	2014		

Smart-S Mk-2 version for 6 Gowind frigates from France

	2	MIRADOR	EO search/fire control	2009	2013-2014	2

For modernization of 2 FS-1500 (Kasturi) frigates

	24	SQUIRE	Ground surv radar	(2011)		

For 24 Pars (AV-8) APC from Turkey

Norway

R: Malaysia	(100)	NSM	Anti-ship missile	(2015)		

For 6 Combat Gowind (SGVP-LCS) frigates

Poland

R: Malaysia	3	MID-M	AEV	2003	2010	3

Part of $368-400 m deal (offsets $111 m)

	5	PMC-90	ABL	2003	2007-2010	(5)

Part of $368-400 m deal (offsets $111 m); PMC Leguan version

	48	PT-91M	Tank	2003	2007-2010	48

Part of $368-400 m deal (offsets $111 m); PT-91M version; Malaysian designation Pendekar

	6	WZT-4	ARV	2003	2007-2010	(6)

Part of $368-400 m deal (offsets $111 m)

Russia

R: Malaysia	(150)	Kh-31A1/AS-17	Anti-ship missile/ARM	(2003)	2007-2009	(150)

Kh-31A and Kh-31P version; for Su-30MKM combat aircraft

	(150)	R-27/AA-10	BVRAAM	(2003)	2007-2009	(150)

R-27RE (AA-10C) version; for Su-30MKM combat aircraft

	(250)	R-73/AA-11	SRAAM	(2003)	2007-2009	(250)

For Su-30MKM combat aircraft

	18	Su-30MK	FGA aircraft	2003	2007-2009	18

$900 m deal (offsets over 33% incl $270 m as barter and incl space technology transfer and training of Malaysian astronaut); Su-30MKM version

	35	RVV-AE/AA-12 Adder	BVRAAM	2012	2012-2013	(35)

$35 m deal

South Africa

R: Malaysia	216	Ingwe	Anti-tank missile	2012	2016	(40)

Part of EUR340 m deal; for Pars (AV-8) IFV

	123	LCT-30	IFV turret	2012		

Part of EUR340 m deal; for Pars IFV from Turkey

| | 54 | MCT | APC turret | 2012 | | |

Part of EUR340 m deal; for PARS APC from Turkey

| | 54 | Rogue | APC turret | 2012 | | |

For 54 Pars (AV-8) APC from Turkey

South Korea

| **R:** Malaysia | 2 | Gagah Samudera | OPV/Training ship | 2011 | | |

MYR294 m deal; delivery 2017

| | 6 | MSC | Frigate | 2014 | | |

$1.2 b deal; incl 3 assembled/produced in Malaysia; delivery from 2018

| | (20) | Barracuda | APC | (2009) | 2009 | (20) |

For police

Spain

| **R:** Malaysia | 1 | Scorpene | Submarine | 2002 | 2009 | 1 |

Part of EUR1.2 b deal (incl 1 more from France; incl over 50% barter)

| | 4 | A400M Atlas | Transport aircraft | 2005 | 2015-2016 | 3 |

EUR500 m deal (offsets at least EUR400 m); incl for air-refueling role; delivery 2015-2017

Sweden

| **R:** Malaysia | 6 | SAK-70 Mk-2 57mm | Naval gun | 2013 | | |

$57 m deal; SAK-70 Mk-3 version; for 6 Gowind frigates from France; probably including assembly and/or production of components in Malaysia

Switzerland

| **R:** Malaysia | 10 | PC-7 Turbo Trainer | Trainer aircraft | 2006 | 2007 | 10 |

CHF70 m deal; PC-7 Mk-2 version

| | 5 | PC-7 Turbo Trainer | Trainer aircraft | (2014) | 2016 | 5 |

PC-7 Mk-2 version

Thailand

| **R:** Malaysia | 20 | First Win | APC/APV | 2015 | 2016 | (10) |

Incl assembly in Malaysia; Malaysian designation AV4 Lipanbara; delivery 2016-2017

Turkey

| **R:** Malaysia | 89 | Pars | APC | 2011 | 2016 | (40) |

Part of MYR7.6 b ($2.5 b) deal; AV8 version; delivery 2016-2019/2020

| | 46 | Pars IFV-25 | IFV | 2011 | 2014-2016 | (40) |

Part of MYR7.6 b ($2.5 b) deal; AV8 version; delivery probably 2014-2018/2019

| | 8 | ACV-S | APC | (2008) | 2010 | 8 |

Part of $153 m deal; mortar carrier version; Malaysian designation Adnan

| | 28 | AIFV | IFV | 2008 | 2010 | 28 |

Part of $153 m deal; ACV-300 version; Malaysian designation Adnan

| | 20 | AIFV-APC | APC | 2008 | 2010 | 20 |

Part of $153 m deal; ACV-300 version; incl 4 anti-tank, 2 CP and 14 ARV versions; Malaysian designation Adnan

| | 122 | Pars IFV-30 | IFV | 2011 | | |

Part of MYR7.6 b ($2.5 b) deal; AV8 version; delivery probably 2017-2019/2020

UAE

| **R:** Malaysia | (4) | Yabhon Aludra | UAV | 2008 | 2008 | (4) |

Lease via Malaysian company; for coastal surveillance

United Kingdom

| **R:** Malaysia | (3) | Jernas | SAM system | 2002 | 2005-2007 | (3) |

GBP220 m ($400 m) deal (offsets incl production of components in Malaysia)

| | (150) | Rapier-2 | SAM | 2002 | 2005-2007 | (150) |

Offsets incl production of components in Malaysia); for Jernas SAM systems

| | (50) | Sea Skua | Anti-ship missile | 2001 | 2007 | (50) |

For Lynx helicopters

| | (3) | Blindfire | Fire control radar | 2002 | 2006-2007 | (3) |

For Jernas SAM system

| | 8 | Viper | Turbojet | 2006 | 2009 | 8 |

For 8 MB-339CM trainer aircraft from Italy; from Italian production line

31	Seawolf	SAM	2007	2010	(31)

MYR186 m ($57 m) deal; Malaysian missiles rebuilt in UK

(1)	Forceshield	SAM system	2015	2016	(1)
(120)	Starstreak	Portable SAM	2015	2016	(120)

For Forcefield SAM system

United States

R: Malaysia

Qty	Designation	Description	Order	Delivery	No.
12	Caterpillar-3616	Diesel engine	2000	2006-2010	(12)

For 6 MEKO-A100 (Kedah) frigates from FRG

| 4 | CT7 | Turboprop | 2002 | 2005-2006 | (4) |

For 2 CN-235 transport aircraft from Indonesia; CT-7-9C3 version

| 20 | AIM-120C AMRAAM | BVRAAM | (2005) | 2007 | (20) |

AIM-120C-5 version

| 4 | RGM-84 Harpoon | Anti-ship missile | (2005) | 2006-2007 | 4 |

AGM-84A version

| 56 | 6V-53 | Diesel engine | 2008 | 2010 | (56) |

For 56 AIFV (ACV-300) IFV/APC from Turkey

| 50 | JDAM | Guided bomb | 2009 | 2011 | (50) |
| (60) | Paveway | Guided bomb | 2010 | 2011 | (60) |

GBU-10 and GBU-12 Paveway-2 versions

| 6 | ASQ-228 ATFLIR | Aircraft EO system | 2012 | 2016 | (3) |

$26 m deal; for modernization of 6 F/A-18D combat aircraft

| 4 | RDR-1700 | MP aircraft radar | (2012) | 2014 | (4) |

For modernization of 4 King Air-200T MP aircraft

| (2) | ScanEagle | UAV | 2012 | 2013 | (2) |

MYR10 m ($3.3 m) lease via Malaysian company; for coastal surveillance

| 20 | AIM-9X Sidewinder | SRAAM | 2013 | 2015 | (20) |

$12 m deal; AIM-9X Block-2 version

| (20) | 6BT | Diesel engine | 2015 | 2016 | (10) |

For 20 First Win APC from Thailand; designation uncertain (reported as '200-300hp Cummins diesel')

| (24) | M-109A5 155mm | Self-propelled gun | 2016 | | |

Second-hand; delivery probably 2017

| 6 | MD-500E | Light helicopter | 2016 | 2016 | (3) |

Armed MD-530MG version; delivery 2016-2017

Brunei

Images/pixabay.com/Brunei flag

The Brunei armed forces are relatively small when compared to its neighbours. It is also geared towards protecting its territorial integrity and its areas of interest. It has 7,000 personnel with 700 reserves. It's defence budget amounts to $0.402 billion. By 2017, Brunei has 20 Light Tanks and 45 AIFV/APCs. The table below shows the weapons procured from the period 2006 – 2016.

Brunei's weapon procurement

Source: SIPRI Arms Transfers Database[72]

---

[72] SIPRI Arms Transfers Database - http://armstrade.sipri.org/armstrade/page/trade_register.php

Supplier/ recipient (R)	No. ordered	designation	Weapon description	Year(s) Weapon of order	Year delivery	of delivered
Denmark						
R: Brunei	3	Scanter-4100	Air/sea search radar	(2007)	2011	3
For 3 OPV-80 (Darussalam) corvettes from FRG						
	1	Scanter-4100	Air/sea search radar	(2012)	2014	1
For 1 OPV-80 (Darussalam) corvette from FRG						
France						
R: Brunei	(24)	Mistral	Portable SAM	2000	2005-2006	(24)
	(20)	MM-40-3 Exocet	Anti-ship MI/SSM	2010	2012	(20)
For OPV-80 (Darussalam) corvettes						
	(10)	MM-40-3 Exocet	Anti-ship MI/SSM	(2012)	2014	(10)
For OPV-80 (Darussalam) corvettes						
Germany (FRG)						
R: Brunei	4	FPB-41	Patrol craft	(2007)	2009-2010	4
Bruneian designation Ijhtihad						
	3	OPV-80	Corvette	2007	2011	3
Bruneian designation Darussalam						
	1	Mustead	Patrol craft	2010	2011	1
From Malaysian production line; Bruneian designation Mustead						
	(1)	OPV-80	Corvette	(2012)	2014	1
Bruneian designation Darussalam						
Netherlands						
R: Brunei	3	STING	Fire control radar	(2007)	2011	3
For 3 OPV-80 (Darussalam) corvettes from FRG; STING Mk-2 version						
	1	STING	Fire control radar	(2012)	2014	1
STING Mk-2 version for 1 OPV-80 (Darussalam) corvette from FRG						
Sweden						
R: Brunei	3	SAK-70 Mk-2 57mm	Naval gun	(2007)	2011	3
For 3 OPV-80 (Darussalam) corvettes from FRG; SAK-70 Mk-3 version						
	(1)	SAK-70 Mk-2 57mm	Naval gun	(2012)	2014	1
SAK-70 Mk-3 version for 1 OPV-80 (Darussalam) corvette from FRG						
United States						
R: Brunei	12	S-70/UH-60L	Helicopter	2011	2013-2015	(12)
S-70i version; from Polish production line						

Vietnam

Images/pixabay.com/Vietnamese flag/army soldiers

The Vietnamese armed forces are geared towards protecting its territorial integrity and its areas of interest. It has 482,000 personnel with 5,000,000 reserves. It's defence budget amounts to $4,01 billion. By 2017, Vietnamese army numbers 412,000 with large reserves. It has 1,270 MBT and 620 Light Tanks and 1,680 AIFV/APCs. The navy has 40,000 personnel 7 submarines and 2 principal surface warship (frigates). The Vietnamese air force has 30,000 personnel with 107 combat aircraft.[73] The table below shows the weapons procured from the period 2006 – 2016.

Vietnam's weapon procurement

Source: SIPRI Arms Transfers Database[74]

Supplier/ recipient (R)	No. ordered	Weapon designation	Weapon description	Year(s) of order	Year of delivery	No. delivered
Belarus						
R: Viet Nam	(5)	S-125T Pechora-2T	SAM system	(2008)	2014-2016	(5)
Vietnamese S-125 (SA-3) rebuilt to S-125TM Pechora-2TM						
Canada						
R: Viet Nam	3	DHC-6	MP aircraft	2010	2014	3
DHC-6-400 Guardian-400 version						
	3	DHC-6 Twin Otter	Transport aircraft	2010	2012-2013	(3)
DHC-6-400 version						
	6	PW100	Turboprop/turboshaft	2014	2014-2015	6
For 3 C-295 transport aircraft from Spain						
Czech Republic						
R: Viet Nam	4	VERA-E	Air search system	(2011)	2014-2016	(4)
France						
R: Viet Nam	2	EC725 Super Cougar	Transport helicopter	(2009)	2011	2
EC-225LP version; for SAR						
India						
R: Viet Nam	4	L&T 35m	Patrol craft	2016		
$100 m deal; for border guard						
Israel						
R: Viet Nam	(150)	RAM	APV	(2006)	2006-2009	(150)
For police; RAM-2000 version						
	(100)	AccuLAR	Guided rocket	(2010)	2014-2016	(100)
	100	EXTRA	Guided rocket/SSM	(2010)	2014-2016	(100)
For coastal defence						
	3	EL/M-2022	MP aircraft radar	(2012)	2014	3
For 3 DHC-6 MP aircraft from Canada (aircraft produced in Canada and modified to MP version in USA with systems from Israel)						
	(2)	EL/M-2288 AD-STAR	Air search radar	2012	2013	(2)
Probably $33 m deal						
	(200)	Derby	BVRAAM	(2015)	2016	(40)
For SPYDER SAM systems						
	(200)	Python-5	BVRAAM	(2015)	2016	(40)
For SPYDER SAM system						
	(5)	SPYDER-MR	SAM system	(2015)	2016	(1)
Romania						
R: Viet Nam	10	Yak-52	Trainer aircraft	2008	2009-2011	(10)
Russia						
R: Viet Nam	(8)	Project-1241/Tarantul	FAC	(2004)	2008-2016	8
Project-12418 (Tarantul-5) version; incl 6 produced in Viet Nam						
	(400)	Igla-1/SA-16	Portable SAM	(1996)	1999-2014	(400)
SA-N-10 version for BPS-500 (Ho-A) and Project-10412 (Svetlyak) patrol craft and probably Project-1241 (Tarantul) FAC						
	(75)	48N6/SA-10D Grumble	SAM	2003	2005-2006	(75)
Part of $200-380 m deal						
	(300)	Kh-35 Uran/SS-N-25	Anti-ship missile	2004	2008-2016	(208)
For Project-11661 (Gepard) frigates and Project-1241 (Tarantul) FAC						

[73] The Military Balance, 01/2017, Volume 117, Issue 1

[74] SIPRI Arms Transfers Database - http://armstrade.sipri.org/armstrade/page/trade_register.php

(200)	9M311/SA-19	SAM	(2006)	2011	(200)

For Kashtan CIWS on 2 Gepard frigates

2	Gepard-3	Frigate	2006	2011	2

Part of $300 m deal; Vietnamese designation Dinh Tien Hoang

(2)	K-300P Bastion-P	Coast defence system	2007	2009-2011	(2)

Part of $300 m deal

4	Project-10412/Svetlyak	Patrol craft	2007	2011-2012	4
2	Project-10412/Svetlyak	Patrol craft	(2007)	2012	2
(40)	Yakhont/SS-N-26	Anti-ship missile	2007	2009-2011	(40)

Part of $300 m deal; for Bastion coastal defence system

(50)	3M-54 Klub/SS-N-27	Anti-ship MI/SSM	(2009)	2013-2016	(50)

For Project-636 (Kilo) submarines; incl 3M14E (SS-N-30B) land-attack version

(80)	53-65 533mm	AS torpedo	(2009)	2013-2016	(80)

For Project-636 (Kilo) submarines

(200)	KAB-500/1500	Guided Bomb	(2009)	2011-2012	(200)
(80)	Kh-31A1/AS-17	Anti-ship missile/ARM	(2009)	2011-2012	(80)

For Su-30MK2 combat aircraft; incl Kh-31P anti-radar version

6	Project-636E/Kilo	Submarine	2009	2013-2016	5

$1.8-2.1 b deal; Project-636M version; Vietnamese designation Ha Noi; delivery 2013-2017

(250)	R-73/AA-11	SRAAM	(2009)	2010-2012	(250)

For Su-30MK2 combat aircraft

8	Su-30MK	FGA aircraft	2009	2010-2011	8

$400-500 m deal; Su-30MK2V version

80	TEST-71	AS/ASW torpedo	(2009)	2013-2016	(80)

For Project-636 (Kilo) submarines

12	Su-30MK	FGA aircraft	2010	2011-2012	12

$1 b deal; Su-30MK2V version

2	Gepard-3	Frigate	2012	2016	(2)
2	Gepard-3	Frigate	2012		

Delivery 2017

12	Su-30MK	FGA aircraft	2013	2014-2016	12

$450-600 m deal; Su-30MK2V version

Slovakia

R: Viet Nam	(2)	P-12/Spoon Rest	Air search radar	(2013)	2014	(2)

Second-hand

	(1)	P-15/Flat Face	Air search radar	(2013)	2014	(1)

Second-hand

Spain

R: Viet Nam	3	C-295	Transport aircraft	2014	2014-2015	3

Ukraine

R: Viet Nam	(16)	DR-76	Gas turbine	(2004)	2008-2016	16

For 8 Project-1241 (Tarantul) FAC from Russia

	(16)	DR-77	Gas turbine	(2004)	2008-2016	(16)

For 8 Project-1241 (Tarantul) FAC from Russia

	(8)	Su-22	FGA aircraft	(2004)	2005-2006	(8)

Second-hand

	4	DT-59	Gas turbine	(2006)	2011	4

For 2 Gepard frigates from Russia

	4	Kolchuga	Air search system	(2009)	2012-2013	(4)

$54 m deal

	4	DT-59	Gas turbine	(2012)	2016	(4)

For 2 Gepard frigates from Russia

	4	DT-59	Gas turbine	2012		

For 2 Gepard frigates from Russia

	(2)	ST-68/Tin Shield	Air search radar	(2012)	2014	(2)

Unknown supplier(s)

R: Viet Nam	(10)	Guardian	APC	(2016)	2016	(10)

USA

Images/pixabay.com/USA flag/F-22 Raptor combat aircraft/ B1-b Bomber/Navy ship destroyer

The US armed forces is one of the largest and leading militaries in the world. It is currently the sole super power that has a global power projection reach. It has state of the art equipment and is a foremost power in the development of innovative military technologies. USA has 1,347,300 personnel, with 865,050 reserves. Its defence budget is a massive $604 billion.

By 2017, the US army numbers 475,350 with 542,550 reserves. It has 2831 MBT (3,500 in store) and 14,289 AIFV/APCs. The navy has 327,750 personnel and 68 submarines and 103 principal surface warships (including 10 aircraft carrier, 23 cruisers, 62 destroyers and 8 frigates).

The US air force has 316,950 personnel with 3,504 combat aircraft (strike and heavy bombers).[75] It has the ability to project powers on a global basis. It has continued to develop and purchase sophisticated state of the art weapons. The table below shows the weapons procured from the period 2006 – 2016.

America's weapon procurement

Source: SIPRI Arms Transfers Database[76]

Supplier/ recipient (R)	No. ordered	designation	Weapon description	Year(s) Weapon of order	Year delivery	of delivered
Australia						
R: United States	1	EPF	Transport ship	2008	2012	1
$185 m deal (part of $1.6 b 'JHSV' (Joint High Speed Vessel) programme)						
	(11)	EPF	Transport ship	2009	2013-2016	6
Part of $1.6 b 'JHSV' (Joint High Speed Vessel) programme						
	3	KC-707	Tanker/transport ac	2011	2011	3
Second-hand; Boeing-707-338C version; owned and operated by US company and leased per hour to US and other armed forces						
Austria						
R: United States	(33)	Pandur	APC	1999	2000-2007	(33)
US designation AGMS (Armored Ground Mobility System)						
	20	DA40	Light aircraft	(2009)	2009	20
Lease; or training; US designation T-52A						
	10	Camcopter S-100	UAV	(2010)	2010-2011	(10)
Ordered for evaluation in 'Yellow Jacket' programme						
Canada						
R: United States	2131	Piranha-3	APC	2000	2002-2007	(2131)
LAV-3 (LAV-25/Stryker) version; incl APC, command post, anti-tank, mortar carrier and MGS FSV versions						
	(704)	Piranha-3	APC	(2005)	2007-2009	(704)

---

[75] The Military Balance, 01/2017, Volume 117, Issue 1

[76] SIPRI Arms Transfers Database - http://armstrade.sipri.org/armstrade/page/trade_register.php

LAV-3 (LAV-25/Stryker) version; incl APC, command post, anti-tank and mortar carrier versions					
615	Piranha-3	APC	2008	2009-2011	(615)
$1.2 b deal; LAV-3 (LAV-25/Stryker) version; incl APC, command post and mortar carrier versions					
352	Piranha-3	APC	2009	2011-2012	(352)
$647 m deal; LAV-3 (LAV-25/Stryker) version; incl APC, command post and mortar carrier versions					
103	Piranha-3	APC	2010	2012	103
$176 m deal; LAV-3 (LAV-25/Stryker) version					
91	Piranha-3	APC	2010	2011-2012	(91)
$143 m deal; LAV-3 (LAV-25/Stryker) version					
292	Piranha-3	APC	2011	2012-2013	(292)
LAV-3 (LAV-25/Stryker SDVH) version					
(748)	PT6	Turboprop/turboshaft	1996	1999-2016	(748)
For 741 PC-9 (T-6A) trainer aircraft from Switzerland; PT-6A-62 version					
3	Global Express	Transport aircraft	2009	2010-2011	(3)
Leased and later bought; modified in USA to communications support aircraft with BACN system; US designation E-11A					
1	Global Express	Transport aircraft	2012	2012	1
$45 m deal; modified in USA to communications support aircraft with BACN system; US designation E-11A					
(4)	PT6	Turboprop/turboshaft	(2014)	2015	(4)
For 4 PC-9 (T-6D) trainer aircraft from Switzerland					

Czech Republic

R: United States	21	L-159A ALCA	FGA aircraft	2014	2015-2016	(7)
Second-hand; for US company for training of US forces					

France

R: United States	44	16PC2.5	Diesel engine	(1996)	2006-2016	40
For 11 San Antonio AALS produced in USA 2006-2017					
(298)	FLASH	ASW sonar	2002	2006-2016	(245)
AQS-22 ALFS version for 298 MH-60R ASW helicopters produced in USA					
(66)	MO-120-RT 120mm	Mortar	2004	2008-2013	(66)
'EFSS' programme; US designation M-327					

Germany (FRG)

R: United States	(346)	EC145	Light helicopter	2006	2006-2015	(346)
$3 b 'LUH' programme (incl 20 years support); US designation UH-72A Lakota					
5	EC145	Light helicopter	(2008)	2009-2010	(5)
US designation H-72A					
(100)	EC145	Light helicopter	2014	2015-2016	(47)
For training; UH-72A or LUH-72A version					
(16)	MTU-1163	Diesel engine	(2003)	2008-2015	10
For 8 Legend (NSC) OPV produced in USA					
(21)	TRS-3D	Air/sea search radar	2004	2006-2016	(10)
TRS-3D/16 version for 12 Freedom (LCS-1) frigates and 8 Legend (NSC) OPV produced in USA and 1 land-based site; possibly incl production in USA					
(15)	Do-328	Transport aircraft	(2009)	2009-2013	(15)
Second-hand; US designation C-146					
6	G-120TP	Trainer aircraft	2015	2016	(6)
For civilian company for training of US military					

Israel

R: United States	(24)	Litening	Aircraft EO system	2005	2006	(24)
Litening-AT version; for F/A-18 combat aircraft; US designation AN/AAQ-28					
6	EL/M-2022	MP aircraft radar	2006	2008-2010	(6)
For modernization of 6 HC-130J MP aircraft; for coast guard					
60	Golan	APC	2007	2007	(60)
$37 m deal; part of 'MRAP-2' programme					
(250)	Litening	Aircraft EO system	2010	2011-2016	(200)
Part of $2.3 b 'ATP-SE' programme; Litening-SE version; delivery 2011-2017					
3	EL/M-2022	MP aircraft radar	2012	2016	(2)
For 3 HC-130J MP aircraft produced in USA; for coast guard; delivery 2016-2017					
(453)	CARDOM 120mm	Mortar	(2002)	2002-2010	(453)
For Stryker (Piranha-3) mortar carrier from Canada					

		K-6 120mm	Mortar	2016		
US designations M-120 and M-121						

Italy

R: United States	21	C-27J Spartan	Transport aircraft	2007	2008-2014	(21)
'JCA' (formerly 'FCA' or 'C-XX') programme; original plan for over 100 reduced to 78, then to 38 and in 2013 to 21						

Japan

R: United States	1	DC-10-40	Transport aircraft	2006	2007	1
Second-hand; modified to tanker aircraft; owned and operated by US company and leased per hour to US and other armed forces						

Jordan

R: United States	21	F-5E Tiger-2	FGA aircraft	2016	2016	(5)
Second-hand; for US company for training of US forces						

Netherlands

R: United States	1	Stan Patrol-4708	Patrol craft	2008	2012	1
$88 m deal; for coast guard						
	(33)	Stan Patrol-4708	Patrol craft	2009	2012-2016	19
For coast guard						

New Zealand

R: United States	(8)	A-4K Skyhawk-2	FGA aircraft	2012	2012	8
Second-hand; for US company for training of US armed forces						
	20	J-52	Turbojet	2012	2012	20
Second-hand; spare for A-4K combat aircraft						
	9	MB-339C	Trainer/combat ac	2012	2012	9
Second-hand; for US company for training of US armed forces						

Norway

R: United States	6500	Protector	APC turret	2007	2007-2010	(6500)
'CROWS-2' programme; M-153 version; for Piranha (Stryker) APC from Canada and other armoured vehicles produced in USA and modernization of M-1 tank						
	(3849)	Protector	APC turret	2009	2010-2012	(3849)
Part of 'CROWS-2' programme; M-153 version						
	(1141)	Protector	APC turret	2011	2012	(1141)
$120 m deal; part of 'CROWS-2' programme; M-153 version						
	(3000)	Protector	APC turret	2012	2013-2015	(3000)
$970 m 'CROWS-3' programme; M-153 version						
		Protector MC	IFV turret	2016		
$329 m deal; for modernization of Stryker (Piranha) IFV						

Poland

R: United States	9	M28 Skytruck	Light transport ac	2009	2009-2011	(9)
US designation C-145A						
	(5)	M28 Skytruck	Light transport ac	(2011)	2012	(5)
US designation C-145A						
	21	MiG-21bis	Fighter aircraft	(2012)	2013	21
Second-hand; for US company for training of US forces						
	4	MiG-21PFM	Fighter aircraft	2012	2013	4
Second-hand; MiG-21UM version; for US company for training of US forces						

Russia

R: United States	6	Mi-8MT/Mi-17	Transport helicopter	(2009)	2012	(6)
Second-hand; for training						

Saudi Arabia

R: United States	1	Boeing-707	Transport aircraft	2005	2006	1
Second-hand; modified to tanker aircraft; owned and operated by US company and leased per hour to US and other armed forces						

South Africa

R: United States	(1311)	RG-31 Nyala	APC	(2003)	2004-2008	(1311)
Mainly for use in Iraq and Afghanistan; incl production in USA and from Canadian production line						

773	RG-31 Nyala	APC	2008	2009-2010	(773)

$552 m deal (incl $199 m for 440 produced in South Africa and $353 m for 333 produced in USA); mainly for use in Afghanistan

250	RG-31 Nyala	APC	2010	2010	(250)

$227 m deal (incl production of components in USA); RG-31A2 version

27	RG-31 Nyala	APC	2010	2011	27

Probably incl production of components in USA

Spain

R: United States | 18 | CN-235MP | MP aircraft | 2004 | 2007-2014 | (18)

Part of coast guard 'Deepwater-2000' programme; CN-235M-300M/C-235ER version; US designation HC-144; incl production of components and assembly in USA

Sweden

R: United States | (32) | SAK-70 Mk-2 57mm | Naval gun | (2004) | 2008-2016 | 15

For 24 Freedom and Independence (LCS) frigates and 8 Legend (NSC) OPV produced in USA; US designation Mk-110

| | (12) | Giraffe AMB | Air search radar | (2004) | 2010-2016 | (5) |

Sea Giraffe AMB version for 12 Independence (LCS-2) frigates produced in USA; US designation SPS-77

Switzerland

R: United States | 748 | PC-9 | Trainer aircraft | 1996 | 1999-2016 | (748)

$7 b 'JPATS' programme (incl $4.7 b for aircraft only); US designation T-6A and T-6B Texan-2

| | (44) | F-5E Tiger-2 | FGA aircraft | 2003 | 2003-2008 | (44) |

Second-hand; $19 m deal; incl 3 F-5F version; for use as 'enemy' in training; US designation F-5N

| | (15) | Hunter | FGA aircraft | 2004 | 2004-2010 | (15) |

Second-hand; Hunter FGA-58 version; for civilian company for training of US forces

| | 4 | PC-9 | Trainer aircraft | 2013 | 2015 | 4 |

T-6D version

Ukraine

R: United States | (128) | Igla/SA-18 | Portable SAM | (2004) | 2005-2006 | 128

Second-hand; probably for evaluation and training

| | 33 | Strela-3/SA-14 | Portable SAM | (2005) | 2006 | 33 |

Second-hand

| | (295) | Igla-1/SA-16 | Portable SAM | 2006 | 2006 | (295) |

Second-hand

United Kingdom

R: United States | (223) | Hawk-60 | Trainer/combat ac | 1981 | 1990-2009 | (223)

'VTXTS' or 'T-45TS' programme; T-45A and T-45C Goshawk version

| | (1026) | UFH/M-777 155mm | Towed gun | (2000) | 2002-2013 | (1026) |

US designation M-777

| | (275) | L-118 105mm | Towed gun | (2005) | 2006-2013 | (275) |

L-119 version; US designation M-119

| | (179) | Air refuel system | Air refuel system | 2011 | | |

For 179 KC-46 tanker/transport aircraft produced in USA

| | (48) | MT-30 | Gas turbine | 2004 | 2008-2016 | 16 |

For 24 Freedom and Independence (LCS) frigates produced in USA

| | 1 | Air refuel system | Air refuel system | 2005 | 2006 | 1 |

For modification of 1 Boeing-707 transport aircraft to K-707 tanker aircraft owned and operated by US company

| | 22 | Seaspray | MP aircraft radar | 2005 | 2008-2011 | (22) |

Seaspray-7500E version; for modernization of 22 Coast Guard HC-130H MP aircraft

| | 1 | Air refuel system | Air refuel system | 2006 | 2007 | 1 |

For modification of 1 DC-10 transport aircraft to KDC-10 tanker aircraft owned and operated by US company

| | 6 | MT-30 | Gas turbine | 2007 | 2016 | 1 |

For 3 Zumwalt (DDG-1000 or DDX) destroyers produced in USA

| | (642) | AGM-65 Maverick | ASM | (2011) | 2012-2013 | 642 |

Second-hand; status uncertain (possible only for US company)

| | (60) | Pegasus | Turbofan | 2011 | 2012 | (60) |

Second-hand; Pegasus-107 version; spares for AV-8B combat aircraft

Unknown supplier(s)

R: United States | 5 | L-39C Albatros | Trainer aircraft | (2011) | 2012 | (5)

Second-hand; for US company for training of US forces

Singapore

Images/pixabay.com/Singapore flag

The Singapore armed forces (SAF) are geared towards protecting its territorial integrity and its areas of interest. It has 72,500 personnel with 312,500 reserves. It's defence budget amounts to $10,02 billion. By 2017, Singapore army numbers 50,000 with 300,000 reserves. It has 96 MBT and 372 Light Tanks and 2,102 AIFV/APCs. The navy has 9,000 personnel 4 submarines and 6 principal surface warship (frigates). The Singapore air force has 13,500 personnel with 134 combat aircraft.[77] The table below shows the weapons procured from the period 2006 – 2016.

Singapore's weapon procurement

Source: SIPRI Arms Transfers Database[78]

Supplier/ recipient (R)	No. ordered	designation	Weapon description	Year(s) Weapon of order	Year delivery	of delivered
Australia						
R: Singapore	100	R-600	IFV turret	2009	2010-2011	(100)
AUD28 m ($22 m) deal; for Terrex APC/IFV produced in Singapore						
	(35)	R-600	IFV turret	2012	2012-2013	(35)
AUD25 m ($27 m) deal; for Terrex APC/IFV produced in Singapore						
Canada						
R: Singapore	(19)	PT6	Turboprop/turboshaft	2006	2008	19
For PC-21 trainer aircraft from Switzerland; PT-6A-68B version						
Denmark						
R: Singapore	12	Scanter-2001	Sea search radar	(2002)	2007-2009	12
For 6 La Fayette (Formidable) frigates from France						
France						
R: Singapore	6	La Fayette	Frigate	2000	2007-2009	6
$750 m deal (part of $1.6 b 'Project Delta'); incl 5 produced in Singapore; Singaporean designation Formidable						
	(300)	ASTER-15 SAAM	SAM	(2001)	2006-2013	(300)
Part of $1.6 b 'Project Delta'; for La Fayette (Formidable) frigates						
	(5)	EC-120 Colibri	Light helicopter	2005	2006	(5)
Part of SGD120 m (EUR60 m) deal (owned by and leased for 20 years from Singaporean company); for training						
	(3)	Ground Master-200	Air search radar	2012	2012-2013	(3)
	(200)	ASTER-30	SAM	2013		
For SAMP/T SAM system						
	(150)	MICA	BVRAAM	(2013)	2016	(20)
For VL-MICA SAM system on 8 LMV (Independence) corvettes						
	(2)	SAMP/T	ABM/SAM system	2013		
	8	VL-MICA-M	Naval SAM system	2013	2016	1
For 8 LMV (Independence) corvettes produced in Singapore						
	(40)	HIGUARD	APC	(2014)	2014-2015	(40)

---

[77] The Military Balance, 01/2017, Volume 117, Issue 1

[78] SIPRI Arms Transfers Database - http://armstrade.sipri.org/armstrade/page/trade_register.php

(60)	Sherpa	APV	(2014)	2015	60
(16)	EC725 Super Cougar	Transport helicopter	2016		

H-225M version

Germany (FRG)

R: Singapore	24	MTU-8000	Diesel engine	(2000)	2007-2009	24

For 6 La Fayette (Formidable) frigates from France; MTU-8000-M90 version

(8)	BR-710	Turbofan	2007	2009-2011	(8)

For 4 G-550 AEW aircraft from USA and Israel

(19)	Buffel	ARV	(2007)	2010-2011	(19)

Second-hand Leopard-2 tank modified to Buffel ARV

(182)	Leopard-2A4	Tank	2007	2007-2012	(182)

Second-hand but modernized before delivery (possibly incl some for spares only)

(10)	PSB-2	ABL	(2010)	2012-2013	(10)

Probably second-hand but modernized before delivery or second-hand Leopard-2 tanks modified to ABL

16	MTU-4000	Diesel engine	2013	2016	(2)

For 8 LMV (Independence) corvettes produced in Singapore

2	Type-218	Submarine	2013		

Type-218SG version; delivery from 2020; option on 2 more

Israel

R: Singapore	(1500)	Spike-MR/LR	Anti-tank missile	1999	2001-2006	(1500)

$150 m deal; probably Spike-LR version

(5)	Hermes-450	UAV	(2005)	2006-2007	(5)
10	Litening	Aircraft EO system	(2005)	2006-2007	(10)
(50)	OWS-25	IFV turret	(2005)	2006-2007	(50)

For modernization of M-113 APC

(100)	SPICE	Guided bomb	(2006)	2007	(100)
4	EL/W-2085	AEW&C system	2007	2009-2011	4

For 4 G-550 AEW aircraft (aircraft from USA fitted with Israeli AEW system)

(75)	Derby	BVRAAM	(2008)	2011-2012	(75)

For SPYDER SAM system

(75)	Python-5	BVRAAM	(2008)	2011-2012	(75)

For SPYDER SAM system

(2)	SPYDER-SR	SAM system	(2008)	2011-2012	(2)
(10)	Heron	UAV	(2010)	2012-2013	(10)
(2)	EL/M-2083 APR	Air search radar	2012	2016	(2)

For use on aerostat

(2)	EL/M-2084	Air search radar	(2014)	2015-2016	(2)

Italy

R: Singapore	(100)	A244 324mm	ASW torpedo	(2000)	2007-2009	(100)

For Lafayette (Formidable) frigates

6	Super Rapid 76mm	Naval gun	(2000)	2007-2009	6

For 6 La Fayette (Formidable) frigates from France

(50)	Black Shark	AS/ASW torpedo	(2007)	2011-2012	(50)

For Västergotland submarines

12	M-346 Master	Trainer/combat ac	2010	2012-2014	(12)

EUR250 m deal (part of $411 m 'AJT' deal); based in France

8	Super Rapid 76mm	Naval gun	2013	2016	1

For 8 LMV (Independence) corvettes produced in Singapore

Netherlands

R: Singapore	(6)	STIR	Fire control radar	(2011)	2013-2015	(6)

STIR Mk-2 version for 6 La Fayette (Formidable) frigates from France

8	NS-100	Air/sea search radar	2013	2016	1

EUR52 m deal; for 8 LMV (Independence) corvettes produced in Singapore

---

South Africa

R: Singapore		Marauder	APC	(2013)	2016	(20)

PCSV ALV version

Spain

R: Singapore	6	A-330 MRTT	Tanker/transport ac	2014		
Delivery from 2018						

Sweden

R: Singapore	2	Västergotland	Submarine	2005	2011-2012	2
Second-hand but modernized (incl with AIP engines) before delivery; SEK1 b ($128 m) 'Northern Light' deal; Singaporean designation Archer						
	(50)	RBS-70 Mk-3 Bolide	Portable SAM	(2009)	2011	(50)
	6	Giraffe AMB	Air search radar	(2010)	2011-2013	(6)
Sea Giraffe AMB version; for modernization of 6 Victory corvettes						

Switzerland

R: Singapore	19	PC-21	Trainer aircraft	2006	2008	19
Ordered via USA; based in Australia						
	(13)	PiPz-3 Kodiak	AEV	(2012)	2014-2015	(13)
Second-hand Leopard-2 tank chassis rebuilt in Switzerland and Germany to L2-AEV (Kodiak) AEV						

United States

R: Singapore	(730)	Caterpillar-3126	Diesel engine	(2000)	2001-2013	(730)
For 730 Bronco APC produced in Singapore						
	6	EDO-980	ASW sonar	(2000)	2007-2009	6
For 6 Lafayette (Formidable) frigates from France						
	50	AIM-120C AMRAAM	BVRAAM	2004	2006	(50)
$25 m deal; AIM-120C-5 version						
	12	F-15SG	FGA aircraft	2005	2009-2010	(12)
$1 b 'NFRP' or 'Peace Carvin 5' programme						
	6	S-70B/SH-60B Seahawk	ASW helicopter	2005	2009-2010	(6)
SH-70(N) version						
	(24)	AAQ-33 Sniper	Aircraft EO system	(2006)	2009-2012	(24)
For F-15 combat aircraft						
	(100)	AIM-120C AMRAAM	BVRAAM	(2006)	2009-2010	(100)
For F-15SG combat aircraft; AIM-120C-5 version						
	50	JDAM	Guided bomb	(2006)	2009	(50)
	(24)	Tiger Eyes	Aircraft EO system	2006	2009-2012	(24)
For F-15 combat aircraft						
	(200)	AIM-9X Sidewinder	SRAAM	(2007)	2009-2012	(200)
For F-15 combat aircraft						
	12	F-15SG	FGA aircraft	2007	2010-2012	(12)
$1 b deal						
	4	G-550 AEW	AEW&C aircraft	2007	2009-2011	4
Ordered and delivered via Israel; AEW systems fitted in Israel						
	(84)	Paveway	Guided bomb	(2007)	2009-2011	(84)
Incl 28 GBU-10 and 56 GBU-12 version						
	(20)	AAQ-33 Sniper	Aircraft EO system	2008	2010-2011	(20)
For F-16 combat aircraft						
	(60)	AGM-154 JSOW	Guided bomb	(2008)	2008-2010	(60)
AGM-154A and AGM-154C version; for F-15SG combat aircraft						
	200	AIM-120C AMRAAM	BVRAAM	(2008)	2013-2016	(200)
AIM-120C-5 and AIM-120C-7 versions						
	(168)	GMLRS	Guided rocket	(2008)	2010-2012	(168)
For HIMARS MRL						
	1	Gulfstream-5	Light transport ac	2008	2012	1
G-550 version; for civilian company for 20 year training of Singaporean air force pilots						
	18	M-142 HIMARS	Self-propelled MRL	2008	2010-2011	(18)
		C-9	Diesel engine	2009	2010-2016	(415)
For AV-81 Terrex (Terrex-1) APC/IFV produced in Singapore						
	35	JDAM	Guided bomb	2009	2010	(35)
	15	MaxxPro	APC	2009	2009	15
MaxxPro Dash version						
	(24)	F-124	Turbofan	2010	2012-2014	(24)
For 12 M-346 trainer/combat aircraft from Italy						
	8	F-15SG	FGA aircraft	(2010)	2013	(8)

				Year(s)		of
670	JDAM	Guided bomb	2010	2011-2012	(670)	
$40 m deal						
(12)	ScanEagle	UAV	(2011)	2012-2013	(12)	
For modernized Victory corvettes						
(124)	Paveway	Guided bomb	(2012)	2014	(124)	
Incl 40 GBU-10 Paveway-2 and 84 GBU-12 Paveway-2 versions						
8	F-15SG	FGA aircraft	(2013)	2014	(8)	
2	S-70B/SH-60B Seahawk	ASW helicopter	2013	2016	2	
100	AIM-120C AMRAAM	BVRAAM	2014	2016	(50)	
AIM-120C-7 version						
20	AIM-9X Sidewinder	SRAAM	2014	2015-2016	(20)	
AIM-9X Block-2 version						
348	GMLRS	Guided rocket	(2014)	2015-2016	(348)	
917	JDAM	Guided bomb	2015	2016	(457)	
(10)	CH-47F Chinook	Transport helicopter	(2016)			
For Army						

Australia

Images/pixabay.com/Australian flag/army soldier/F-18 Super Hornet combat aircraft

The Australian armed forces are geared towards protecting its territorial integrity and its areas of interest. It has 57,800 personnel with 21,100 reserves. It's defence budget amounts to $24.2 billion. By 2017, Australian army numbers 29,000 with 13,200 reserves. It has 59 MBT and 684 AIFV/APCs. The navy has 14,400 personnel 6 submarines and 11 principal surface warship (frigates). The Australian air force has 14,400 personnel with 147 combat aircraft.[79] The table below shows the weapons procured from the period 2006 – 2016.

Australia's weapon procurement

Source: SIPRI Arms Transfers Database

Supplier/ recipient (R)	No. ordered	Weapon designation	Weapon description	Year(s) Weapon of order	Year delivery	of delivered
Canada						
R: Australia	(49)	PT6	Turboprop/turboshaft	(2015)		
France						
R: Australia	22	EC-665 Tiger	Combat helicopter	2001	2004-2011	(22)
	(300)	MU90 IMPACT	ASW torpedo	2003	2008-2016	(270)
	12	NH-90 TTH	Transport helicopter	2005	2007-2010	(12)
	35	NH-90 TTH	Transport helicopter	2006	2011-2016	(30)
	12	Barracuda	Submarine	2016		
	12	TSM-2633 Spherion-B	ASW sonar	1989	1996-2009	12
	17	Vampyr	Air search system	2005	2010-2015	(11)
	2	Vampyr	Air search system	(2009)	2014-2015	2
	24	FLASH	ASW sonar	2011	2013-2016	24
	2	Air refuel system	Air refuel system	2015		

[79] The Military Balance, 01/2017, Volume 117, Issue 1

Germany (FRG)

R: Australia	8	MEKO-200ANZ	Frigate	1989	1996-2006	8
	(259)	Waran	APC	2002	2007-2011	(259)
	(144)	DM-702 SMART-155	Guided shell	2007	2008	144
	4	MAN-3240	Diesel engine	(2007)	2014-2015	4
	(81)	Waran	APC	2008	2011-2012	(81)
	15	EC135	Light helicopter	2014	2015-2016	(15)

Ireland

R: Australia	299	Bushmaster	APC	(1999)	2005-2007	(299)
	144	Bushmaster	APC	2006	2007-2008	(144)
	(253)	Bushmaster	APC	2007	2008-2010	(253)
	41	Bushmaster	APC	2008	2010	(41)
	101	Bushmaster	APC	2011	2012	(101)
	214	Bushmaster	APC	2012	2012-2014	(214)

Israel

R: Australia	37	Litening	Aircraft EO system	2005	2006-2007	(37)
	(10)	RecceLite	Aircraft recce system	(2007)	2009-2010	(10)
	(10)	Heron	UAV	2009	2009	(10)

Italy

R: Australia	2	A-109K	Light helicopter	(2006)	2007	(2)
	10	C-27J Spartan	Transport aircraft	2012	2015-2016	(10)

Norway

R: Australia	(59)	Protector	APC turret	(2006)	2007	(59)
	1	Skandi Bergen	OPV	2012	2012	1

South Korea

R: Australia	1	Delos	Tanker	2004	2006	1

Spain

R: Australia	5	A-330 MRTT	Tanker/transport ac	2004	2011-2012	(5)
	2	BPE	AALS	2007	2014-2015	2
	3	Hobart	Destroyer	2007		
	2	Cantabria	Oiler	2016		

Sweden

R: Australia	8	CEROS-200	Fire control radar	(1991)	1996-2006	8
	8	Sea Giraffe-150	Air search radar	1991	1996-2006	8
	(150)	RBS-70 Mk-3 Bolide	Portable SAM	2003	2003-2007	(150)
	2	Giraffe AMB	Air search radar	(2009)	2014-2015	2
	3	Giraffe AMB	Air search radar	2010	2012-2013	3

Switzerland

R: Australia	49	PC-21	Trainer aircraft	(2015)		

United Kingdom

R: Australia	5	Air refuel system	Air refuel system	2004	2011-2012	(5)
	35	UFH/M-777 155mm	Towed gun	(2010)	2012	35
	(20)	ASRAAM	SRAAM	(2011)	2012	20
	1	Enforcer	AALS	2011	2011	1
	19	UFH/M-777 155mm	Towed gun	2012	2014-2015	(19)
	2	Air refuel system	Air refuel system	2015		

United States

R: Australia	4	Boeing-737 AEW&C	AEW&C aircraft	2000	2009-2010	4
	(600)	RIM-162 ESSM	SAM	2002	2003-2016	(480)
	2	Boeing-737 AEW&C	AEW&C aircraft	2004	2011-2012	2
	(72)	F-35A JSF	FGA aircraft	(2009)	2014	2
	(250)	JDAM	Guided bomb	2011	2015-2016	(250)
	12	P-8A Poseidon	ASW aircraft	2014	2016	1
	8	LM-2500	Gas turbine	(1989)	1996-2006	8
	8	Mk-45 127mm	Naval gun	(1989)	1996-2006	8

8	SPS-49	Air search radar	1993	1996-2006	8
(299)	Caterpillar-3126	Diesel engine	(1999)	2005-2007	(299)
(250)	AIM-120B AMRAAM	BVRAAM	(2000)	2001-2006	(250)
(70)	AGM-142A/Popeye-1	ASM	(2001)	2005-2008	(70)
4	Mk-41	Naval SAM system	(2002)	2006-2008	4
64	RGM-84L Harpoon-2	Anti-ship MI/SSM	2002	2006-2014	(64)
(676)	FGM-148 Javelin	Anti-tank missile	2003	2005-2007	(676)
(150)	Mk-48 Mod-5 ADCAP	AS/ASW torpedo	(2003)	2007-2010	(150)
5	PSTAR-ER	Air search radar	2003	2004-2006	(5)
10	CF-6/F-103	Turbofan	(2004)	2011-2012	10
59	M-1A1 Abrams	Tank	2004	2006-2007	59
7	M-88A2 HERCULES	ARV	2004	2006-2007	7
(100)	JDAM	Guided bomb	2005	2007-2008	(100)
3	King Air	Light transport ac	2005	2005-2006	3
(175)	Standard Missile-2MR	SAM	(2005)	2008-2014	(175)
(12)	T55-L	Turboshaft	(2005)	2006-2008	(12)
(500)	AGM-114K HELLFIRE	Anti-tank missile	2006	2006-2009	(500)
(260)	AGM-158A JASSM	ASM	(2006)	2011-2014	(260)
4	C-17A Globemaster-3	Heavy transport ac	2006	2006-2008	4
(144)	Caterpillar-3126	Diesel engine	2006	2007-2008	(144)
3	Mk-41	Naval SAM system	2006		
(50)	AGM-154 JSOW	Guided bomb	(2007)	2009-2016	(50)
(24)	ASQ-228 ATFLIR	Aircraft EO system	(2007)	2010-2011	(24)
(253)	Caterpillar-3126	Diesel engine	2007	2008-2010	(253)
24	F/A-18E Super Hornet	FGA aircraft	2007	2010-2011	24
(4)	ScanEagle	UAV	2007	2007	(4)
3	Type-2150	ASW sonar	(2007)		
47	AIM-9X Sidewinder	SRAAM	2008	2009-2010	(47)
(41)	Caterpillar-3126	Diesel engine	2008	2010	(41)
(8)	F414	Turbofan	2008	2010-2011	(8)
2	LM-2500	Gas turbine	2008	2014-2015	2
250	M-982 Excalibur	Guided shell	2008	2009	(250)
3	SPY-1F	Air search radar	2008		
5	King Air	Light transport ac	(2009)	2010	5
3	SPQ-9	Fire control radar	2009		
3	Mk-45-4 127mm	Naval gun	(2010)		
(10)	RQ-7 Shadow-200	UAV	2010	2011-2012	(10)
3	Bell-429	Light helicopter	2011	2012	3
1	C-17A Globemaster-3	Heavy transport ac	2011	2011	1
(101)	Caterpillar-3126	Diesel engine	2011	2012	(101)
2	CH-47D Chinook	Transport helicopter	2011	2012	2
24	MH-60R Seahawk	ASW helicopter	2011	2013-2016	24
(20)	AE-2100	Turboprop	2012	2015-2016	(20)
1	C-17A Globemaster-3	Heavy transport ac	2012	2012	1
(214)	Caterpillar-3126	Diesel engine	2012	2012-2014	(214)
7	CH-47F Chinook	Transport helicopter	2012	2015	7
(200)	Mk-54 MAKO	ASW torpedo	2012	2013-2016	(200)
(600)	AGM-114K HELLFIRE	Anti-tank missile	(2013)	2014-2016	(600)
110	AIM-120C AMRAAM	BVRAAM	(2013)	2015-2016	(110)
12	EA-18G Growler	FGA/EW aircraft	2013	2015-2016	(8)
(1000)	M-1156 PGK	Guided shell	(2013)	2016	(250)
(7)	MQ-4C Triton	UAV	(2013)		
	AIM-9X Sidewinder	SRAAM	(2014)		
3	F414	Turbofan	2014	2016	(3)
(9)	Mk-15 Phalanx	CIWS	(2014)	2015-2016	(4)
(16)	AGM-88E AARGM	ARM	2015	2016	(8)
1	Bell-429	Light helicopter	(2015)	2016	1
2	C-17A Globemaster-3	Heavy transport ac	2015	2015	2
2	G-550 SIGINT	SIGINT aircraft	2015		

New Zealand

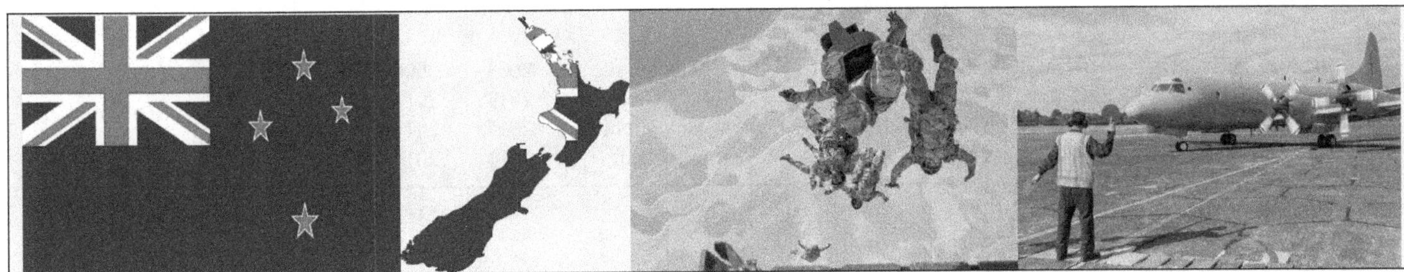

Images/pixabay.com/New Zealand flag/Special forces

The New Zealand armed forces are geared towards protecting its territorial integrity and its areas of interest. It has 8,950 personnel with 2,200 reserves. It's defence budget amounts to $2,58 billion. By 2017, New Zealand army numbers 4,500 with 1,550 reserves. It has 95 AIFV/APCs. The navy has 2,050 personnel and 2 principal surface warship (frigates). The New Zealand air force has 2,400 personnel with 6 combat aircraft.[80] The table below shows the weapons procured from the period 2006 – 2016.

New Zealand's weapon procurement

Source: SIPRI Arms Transfers Database

Supplier/ recipient (R)	No. ordered	No. designation	Weapon description	Year(s) Weapon of order	Year delivery	of delivered
Australia						
R: New Zealand	2	Tenix-1600	OPV	2004	2010	2
	4	Tenix-340	Patrol craft	2004	2009	4
	..	Penguin-2	Anti-ship missile	2013	2014-2016	(30)
Canada						
R: New Zealand	(11)	PT6	Turboprop/turboshaft	2014	2014-2015	(11)
Finland						
R: New Zealand	2	W-18	Diesel engine	2000	2007	2
France						
R: New Zealand	9	NH-90 TTH	Transport helicopter	2006	2011-2014	9
Germany (FRG)						
R: New Zealand	4	MAN-280	Diesel engine	2004	2010	4
Israel						
R: New Zealand	6	EL/M-2022	MP aircraft radar	2005	2011-2014	(6)
Italy						
R: New Zealand	5	A-109K	Light helicopter	2008	2011-2012	(5)
	3	A-109K	Light helicopter	2010	2012	3
Netherlands						
R: New Zealand	1	MRV	AALS	2004	2007	1
	2	PAGE	Air search radar	2004	2006	2
	2	SMART	Air search radar	2014		

South Korea

---

[80] The Military Balance, 01/2017, Volume 117, Issue 1

R: New Zealand	1	Polar	Support ship	2016		
United Kingdom						
R: New Zealand	. .	CAMM	SAM	2014		
United States						
R: New Zealand	(164)	FGM-148 Javelin	Anti-tank missile	2003	2006-2008	(164)
	8	SH-2G Super Seasprite	ASW helicopter	2013	2014-2015	8
	(10)	FGM-148 Javelin	Anti-tank missile	2014	2014	(10)
	11	PC-9	Trainer aircraft	2014	2014-2015	11

Force Multipliers

Image/pixabay.com/USA military aircraft carriers/firepower

Technology

Technological innovations in military technology have had a profound effect on strategy and the ability to have an edge in any conflict. Technology has given better situational awareness and long range precision strikes. State of the art offensive and defensive weapons have given the impetus for a new range of strategies and tactics.[81]

Image/pixabay.com/anti-tank guided missile/T72 main battle tank

Images/pixabay.com/ v-22-osprey-boeing-helicopter/amphibian assault battalion convoy

Images/pixabay.com/USMC amphibious training/CH-53 Super stallion helicopter

[81] J.Goldstein & J. Pevehouse, International Relations, United States, 2007

Images/pixabay.com/F-15 Eagle combat aircraft/soldier training

Images/pixabay.com/army rangers parachuting/Hawkeye radar-aircraft-squadron

Network-Centric Warfare

Images/pixabay.com/monitor binary system/radar protection/US navy radar technicians/satellite communications

Network-centric warfare is a combination of factors that have enabled states to gain information on their adversaries. Network-centric seeks to gain an information advantage by the use of sophisticated information technology, into a competitive advantages through the use of computer networking of geographically dispersed forces. It allows all parties at different levels to be well informed. This level of coordination and information could be detrimental to any force.

In addition to this, the important emerging field of Information and Cyberwarfare that involves the battlespace use of computers and networks in warfare (tactical information, cyberattacks, espionage and sabotage). The importance of the use of an ever changing Battlespace can be essential in unifying military strategy to integrate and combine armed forces for the military theatre of operations (including air, information, land, sea, cyber and space to achieve military goals). The countries in the East Asian region are developing or improving these vital technologies.[82]

Tankers

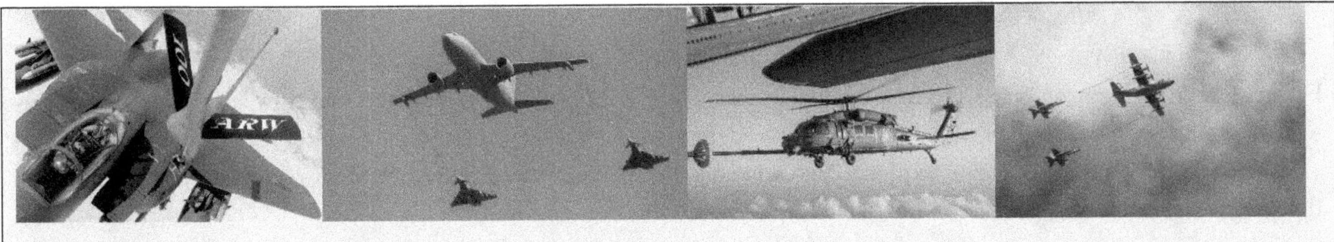

Images/pixabay.com/air to air refuelling/tankers/helicopter refuelling/Hercules tanker refuelling

Air to air refuelling by tankers have resulted an increase in the rage of combat aircraft. It has also allowed Combat patrol aircraft to extend its range and hence stay on patrol without having to land and refuel. The tankers have increased the range and loitering time within or near the designated target areas. It also allows fighter and bomber aircraft to carry extra weapons/bombs instead of extra fuel tanks.

Tankers are considered force multiplier aircraft as they allow fighter, bombers, special mission aircraft, transport aircraft to be rapidly deploy to the areas where they are needed.

Bombers

Images/pixabay.com/B1b bomber/B2 Spirit/F-15 Eagles and B1b bomber in South Korea

---

[82] J.Goldstein & J. Pevehouse, International Relations, United States, 2007

Bombers with precision guided bombs and missiles have been able to attack targets without the support of other aircraft such as, the need for large escort fighter aircraft, electronic warfare aircraft etc. Precision guided munitions (PGM) have given an attacking force the ability to strike with pin-point accuracy.

AWACS/Special Mission Aircraft

Images/pixabay.com/E3 Sentry/Self-defence/maritime aircraft

Fighter aircraft have been given significant support from an AWACS platform. Fighters can now approach targets without being revealed by their own radar. They can defend and strike key areas with higher confidence. Enemy aircraft or air defence systems can be picked up earlier by the AWACS aircraft and the information is given to the fighter aircrafts a lot earlier, thereby minimising the risks to the fighter aircraft.[83]

Stealth

Images/pixabay.com/B2 Stealth bomber/F22 Stealth fighter/F-35 Stealth fighter/Russian T50 Pakfa stealth aircraft

Stelath technologies have given certain countries the ability to force multiply their military power. Stealth aircraft have a special design that reduces its chance of being detected by an adversary forces. It allows countries to undertake very dangerous missions in which a highly protected area can taken out with military precision and the chance of the aircraft surving is high. These technologies can be seen as game changing weapons that can cause substantial losses to an adversary with minimum losses to the launching nation. The Wars in Iraq and Bosnia had indicated the lethality of stealth.

UCAV/UAV

---

[83] J.Goldstein & J. Pevehouse, International Relations, United States, 2007

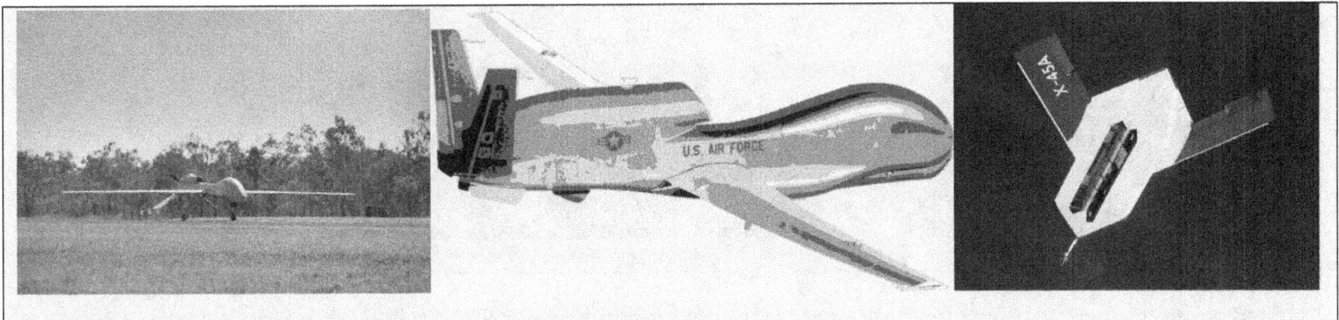

Images/pixabay.com/MQ-1c Predator drone/Global Hawk UAV drone/boeing-x-45a-aircraft-drone

Drones have become sophisticated and can be used for a number of operations, such as surveillance, gathering intelligence and patrolling airspace/borders/maritime reconnaissance etc. The unmanned combat aerial vehicle (UCAV) also known as combat drones, usually carry smart munitions and missiles to strike at designated targets. The drones are under real-time human control with different levels of autonomy. They are cheaper and safer to operate than manned combat aircraft.[84]

Missiles

Images/pixabay.com/air to air missiles/laser guided bombs/ballistic missiles

Advances in sophisticated missiles ensures that the offensive and defensive use of them can alter the battlefield. Countries are developing and purchasing weapons that have long range strike abilities. Countries can now attack their adversaries at much longer and safer distances. Missiles come in different sizes and shapes and adapted for different purposes: surface-to-surface and air-to-surface missiles (ballistic, cruise, anti-ship, anti-tank, etc.), surface-to-air missiles (and anti-ballistic), air-to-air missiles, beyond visual range (BVR) and anti-satellite weapons. These missiles have altered the scenes of a modern conflict and have given nations a number of choices in their use (stand-off capabilities).

Submarines

---

[84] J.Goldstein & J. Pevehouse, International Relations, United States, 2007

Images/pixabay.com/submarines

Submarines are hunters that operate in the oceans and have a number of roles to fullfill. The main defense of a submarine lies in its ability to remain concealed in the depths of the ocean. A hidden submarine is a real threat, and because of its stealth, can force an enemy navy to waste resources searching large areas of ocean and protecting ships against attack. Submarines operate in different roles, such as anti-shipping and mine-laying. The development of submarine-launched ballistic missile (SLBM) and submarine-launched cruise missiles (SLCM) gave submarines a considerable and long-ranged capability to attack both land and sea targets with a selection of weapons ranging from torpedos, anti-ship, cluster bombs to nuclear weapons. Its purpose to achieve sea-denial for an adversary and to make it costly for an opponent country to attack (deterrence). It is also used for softening enemy targets at the incept of hostillities, as indicated in the Iraq, Bosnia, Afghanistan conflict – US navy Tomahawk long range misiles were used to attack key targets (Command & Control facilities, air defences, radar sites etc.).[85]

Aircraft Carriers

Images/pixabay.com/aircraft carriers/F-18 Super Hornets landing and taking off on carriers

Aircraft carriers are true force multipliers and are a symbol of power projection capabilities of a nation. They are equipped with combat aircraft and helicopters and essentially a floating airbase. It allows countries to send their task force to a desgnated area and use it for air power deployment. It reduces the times and transit distances of aircraft and therefore significantly increase the time of availability on the combat zone. The Aircraft carriers have been used in a devastingly manner in modern warfare. The aircraft carrier allows a naval force to project air power worldwide without depending on local bases for staging aircraft operations (they usually carry numerous sophisticated fighter planes, strike aircraft, helicopters, airborne early warning aircraft and other types of aircraft).

East Asian Nations

A number of force multiplier items are in either development or in the process of purchasing from other countries. These sophisticated weapons will enable adversaries to inflict serious damage to their respective targets. The increased income (GDP) has given the rivals an impetus to purchase these technologies. Hence any future conflict will have devastating effects in the region.[86]

Chapter 4: Weapons of Mass Destruction (WMD)

---

[85] J.Goldstein & J. Pevehouse, International Relations, United States, 2007
[86] J.Goldstein & J. Pevehouse, International Relations, United States, 2007

Image/pixabay.com/North and South Korea/Atomic bomb/Liberty mushroom cloud/US Trump threats/North Korean Kim Jong-Un

Since the end of the Cold War period, nuclear weapons have been reduced from a massive 70,300 warheads in 1986 to an estimated 14,550 bombs in 2017.[87] In 2017 the following nine countries possessed nuclear weapons and all have been developing a number of methods to launch nuclear weapons to deter any would be adversary (land-based intercontinental ballistic missiles, strategic bombers, and submarine-launched ballistic missiles) - the USA, Russia, UK, France, China, India, Pakistan, Israel and North Korea possess nuclear weapons.[88]

All the nuclear powers have either developed or are in the process of developing different technologies to ensure that they are able to deter a would be adversary. New ballistic missiles, air launched cruise missiles (ALCM), ground (GLCM) and sea based nuclear delivery systems are being pursued by the nuclear powers.[89]

Table 1. World nuclear forces, 2017

Country	Year of first nuclear test	Deployed warheads*	Other warheads	Total 2017
USA	1945	1,800	5,000	6,800
Russia	1949	1,950	5,050	7,000
UK	1952	120	95	215
France	1960	280	20	300
China	1964		270	270
India	1974		120–130	120–130
Pakistan	1998		130–140	130–140
Israel	. .		80	80
North Korea	2006		10-20	10-20
Total		**4,150**	**10,785**	**14,935**

* Deployed warheads refers to warheads placed on missiles or located on bases with operational forces. ** Other warheads refers to warheads that are held in reserve or that are retired and awaiting dismantlement. SIPRI Yearbook 2017.

87 https://fas.org/issues/nuclear-weapons/status-world-nuclear-forces/

88 https://www.sipri.org/media/press-release/2017/global-nuclear-weapons-modernization-remains-priority

89 https://www.armscontrol.org/factsheets/Nuclearweaponswhohaswhat

Global nuclear weapons modernisation remains priority

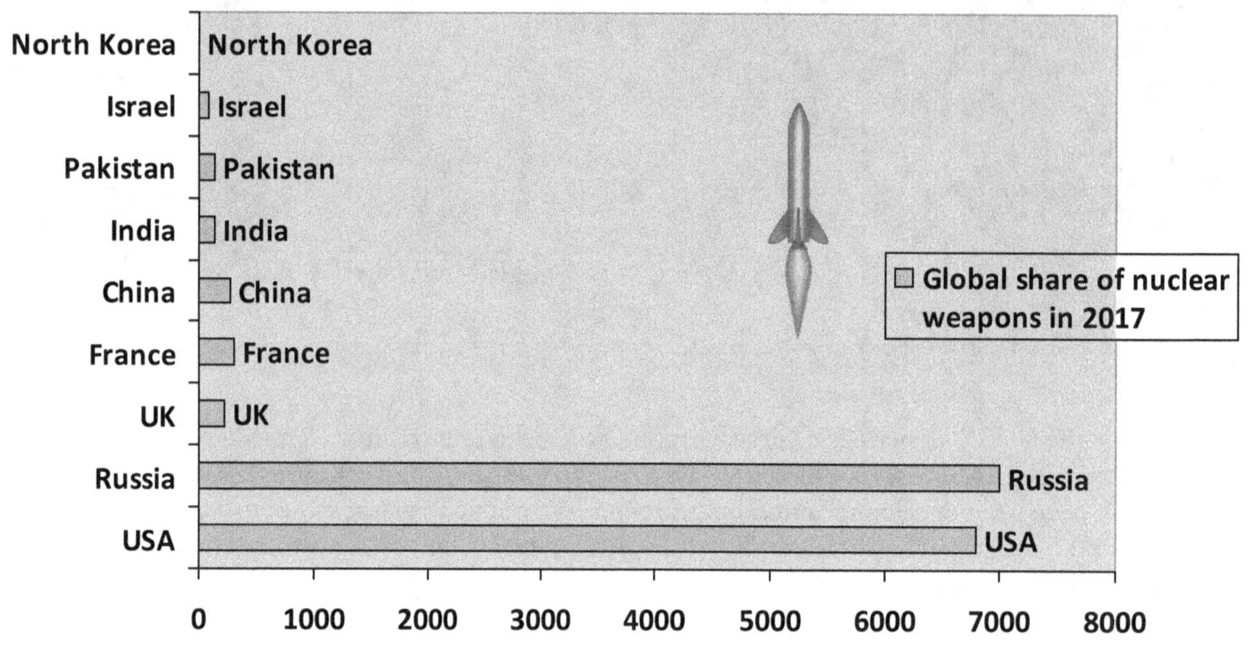

90

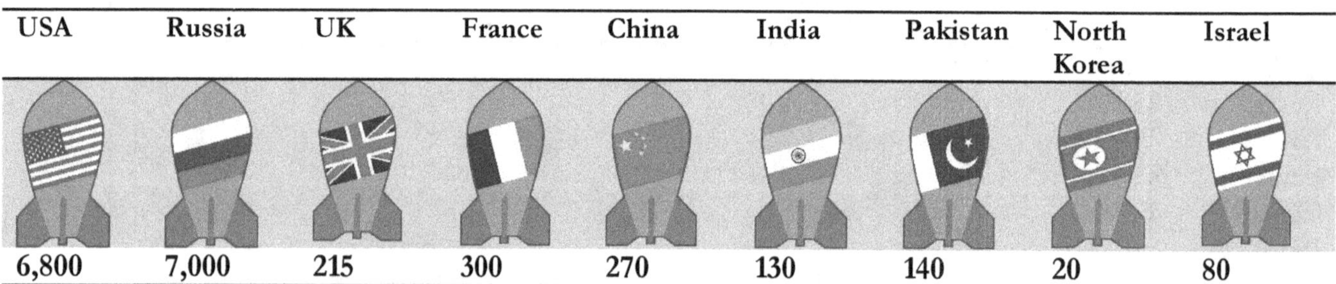

USA	Russia	UK	France	China	India	Pakistan	North Korea	Israel
6,800	7,000	215	300	270	130	140	20	80

https://fas.org/issues/nuclear-weapons/status-world-nuclear-forces/

Weapons of Mass Destruction

The proliferation of weapons of mass destruction (nuclear, biological, and chemical) and the missiles to deliver them pose a significant threat to the countries of East Asia. For instance there is evidence to support that North Korea has the ability to assemble a nuclear device in addition to developing long range nuclear capable ballistic missiles, such as the Nodong and the Taepo Dong 2 which have ranges from 1000km-4000km. Fired from North Korea these missiles could reach a significant part of East Asia including Japan.[91] It has further developed its new improved missiles – the Hwansong that has the capability to strike at US mainland (ICBM).

---

[90] https://www.sipri.org/media/press-release/2017/global-nuclear-weapons-modernization-remains-priority

8.   Bearman, op cit:166

Images/pixabay.com/North Korean Ballistic missiles parade/Ballistic missile test/Military aircraft formation

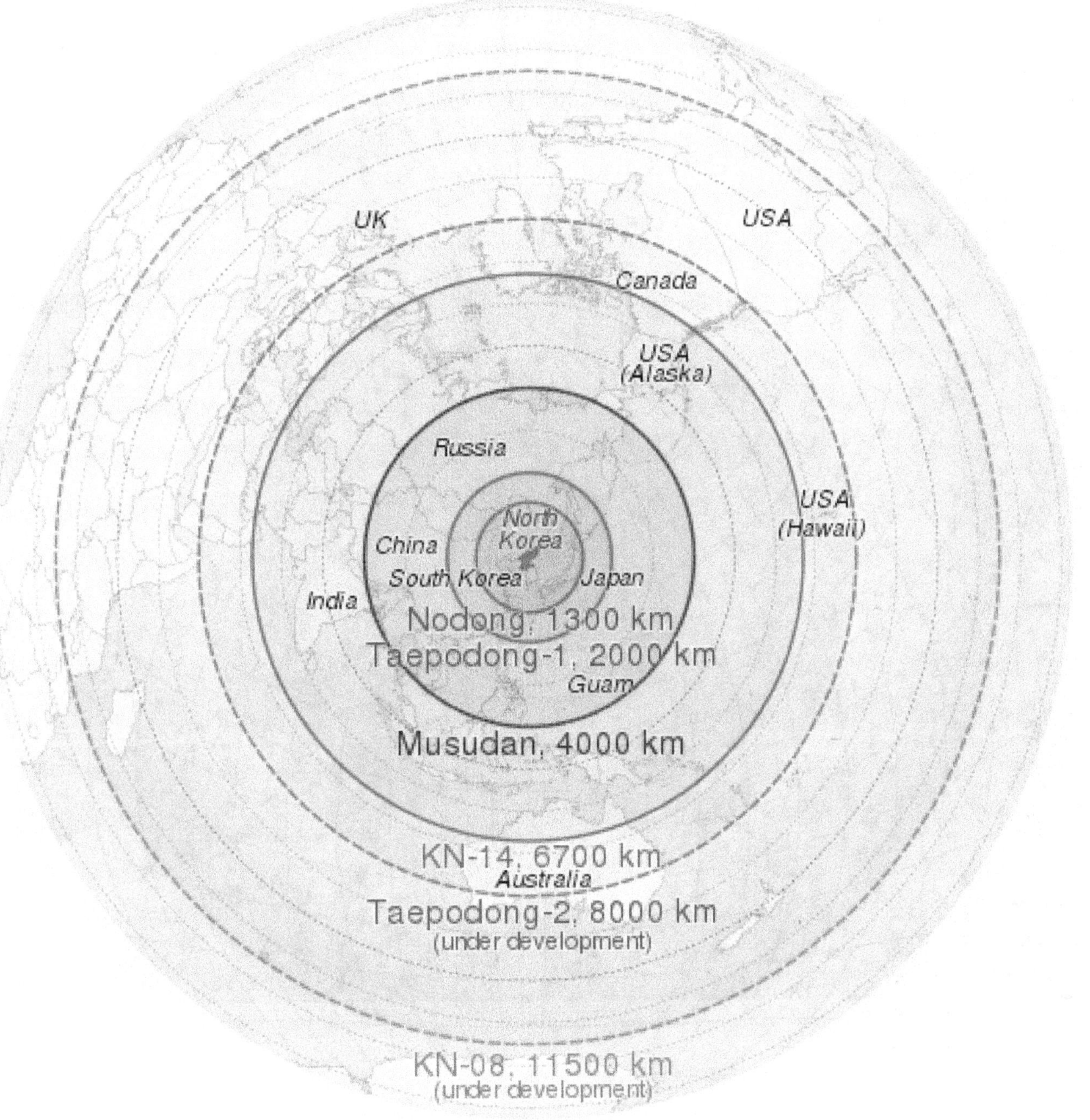

Images/commons.wikimedia.org/North Korean missile range

A Number of territorial disputes also exist in this part of the region such as the claims by China and Taiwan to the Senkaku islands occupied by Japan.[92] Furthermore Japan's neighbours are also alarmed at the Japanese plutonium reprocessing program, in spite of Japanese efforts to demonstrate its intentions to use this capability for civilian energy production, they argue that the Japanese have the capacity to develop nuclear weapons in no more than a few years at most.[93] In addition the North Korean nuclear missile threat has resulted in Japan purchasing a missile defence capability, such as the American 'Patriot' anti-ballistic missile system and there are concerns over reports that if North Korea goes nuclear then Japan will go nuclear as well (as a countermeasure to the North Korean threat). This has caused concern in China that sees Japan as a potential threat in the region.[94]

China has clearly expressed its concern that if Japan obtained a Missile Defense capability, while enhancing Japanese nuclear capabilities (such as its plutonium processing program), then China would take steps to insure the adequacy of their deterrent force, presumably by constructing more nuclear warheads and more missiles. Not only would this response further increase tensions in the region, particularly concerns about China's military strength, it would increase the capacity of the Chinese to be a supplier of WMD, their delivery systems, and their means of production. [95]

Image/pixabay.com/Patriot missile defence

9.   Brown, op cit:86

10. Chalmers, Greene & Zhiqiong, op cit:28

11. Brown, op cit:234

12. Ibid

China & Taiwan

The Chinese dispute over renegade Taiwan has resulted in China refusing to rule out using force against Taiwan, for instance early in the morning of March 8,1996, China fired three nuclear-capable missiles into two areas close to Taiwan as part of missile 'tests', these tests were taking place alongside large-scale Chinese ground and naval exercises in areas near Taiwan. The exercises have featured practicing the largest airborne assault ever conducted by China, as well as a huge amphibious exercise aimed at Taiwan. Thus China and North Korea are the only Asian countries using nuclear-capable missiles to intimidate its neighbours. [96]

North Korean Nuclear and Missile tests

The belligerent stance of North Korea and the USA (including its allies) has further increased tensions in the region. North Korea seas a threat from South Korea which has been backed up by the USA. The have seen the regular military exercise from its opponents and this has further heightened its concerns. The North Korean military apparatus is not strong enough to deter larger sophisticated military powers and hence it began to develop nuclear weapons and its delivery vehicles to reduce US regional hegemony in the area.

Its development of nuclear weapons has alarmed a lot of its neighbours and has resulted in global concern in regards to its nuclear development. North Korea has had a number of sanctions that have been authorised by the United Nations Council (UN) but this has not deterred it from pursuing its goals.[97]

North Korea has tested its sixth nuclear test and has rapidly increased its missile program. In 2017 it had launched 23 missiles during its 16 tests and this has enabled it improve on the technology to ensure reliability and improved capability. It has improved its range and has controversially fired its missiles in Japan's exclusive economic zone. It is improving its short range, medium range missiles and working on an intercontinental ballistic missile (ICBM) missile with reach to target mainland USA.[98]

North Korea intends to deter the USA from attacking its country and undertake a regime change by sending a clear message of its ballistic missile reach of mainland USA. It believes that the USA will not try to topple the North Korean regime of Kim Jung On from power if it new that North Korea is capable of a nuclear attack on the USA mainland. Pyongyang believes Washington would not launch an attack in case of a reprisal and see its nuclear weapons as a deterrence to USA aggression. North Korea is familiar with fall of regimes in Iraq, Libya and elsewhere done by the USA. [99]

The USA see this as a threat and is trying different ways of addressing this issue. The US president, Donal Trump has threatened to "totally destroy" North Korea if his country is forced to defend itself or its allies.[100] North Korean leader Kim Jong-un has described the US president as "mentally deranged".[101]

---

[96] The Economist, **Asian Security**, Published by the Economist Newspaper Ltd, 1996, p83

[97] http://edition.cnn.com/2017/05/29/asia/north-korea-missile-tests/index.html

[98] Joshua Berlinger, CNN December 4, 2017 http://edition.cnn.com/2017/05/29/asia/north-korea-missile-tests/index.html

[99] Joshua Berlinger, CNN December 4, 2017 http://edition.cnn.com/2017/05/29/asia/north-korea-missile-tests/index.html

[100] http://www.bbc.co.uk/news/world-asia-40882877

[101] http://www.bbc.co.uk/news/world-asia-40882877

There are approximately 28,500 US military personnel based in South Korea, divided by the 4km-wide demilitarised zone that stretches more than 250km along the border. The frequent tests of ballistic missiles by the North Korean regime and South Korean military exercises near the border with US forces has increased tensions. The North Korean regime's main goal is survival - and direct conflict with the US would seriously endanger it. A US attack on North Korea would force the North Korean regime to retaliate against US allies South Korea and Japan. This would result in a massive loss of life. In addition, it could also prompt North Korea to fire its nuclear capable ICBM missiles at the US mainland. The rhetoric coming from the North Korean and US leadership could lead to miscalculation from both sides – resulting in a catastrophic conflict in the region.[102]

Therefore, it is vital that confidence building measures are introduced into the region and that tensions are gradually reduced. The region needs to amicably resolve its conflict otherwise, any misinterpreted move in the current tense environment could lead to an accidental war with horrendous results.[103]

---

[102] http://www.aljazeera.com/news/2017/05/north-korea-testing-nuclear-weapons-170504072226461.html

[103] http://www.bbc.co.uk/news/world-asia-40882877

Chapter 5: Confidence Building measures and Summary

Image/pixabay.com/USA Military Aircraft Carriers

On account of the numerous maritime and territorial disputes in the region, which have caused considerable amounts of tension, suspicion, and misunderstandings and also the fact that most of the countries in the region had identified economic prosperity as their overriding concern, it was therefore in the interest of the nations in this region to set up institutions of dialogue which would tackle specific security and economic problems facing the region. [104]

Thus, confidence building measures appear to be taking a foothold in the region For instance various countries have promoted bi-lateral arrangements such as defence-industrial co-operation, security dialogue and closer military ties. In the domain of arms export controls, many East Asian countries have also shown an increasing willingness to submit returns to the UN Register of Conventional Arms. Traditionally, many in the region have been reluctant to disclose data on their military capabilities.[105]

The UN Register of Conventional Arms will permit states to collect significant quantities of data on the production and flow of arms. If most of that data is made available to other governments and to the public, this should directly increases the level of transparency in the region. Not only does this increased transparency reduce uncertainty and suspicion regarding state behavior, but this could also encourage more open, democratic systems (which appear less threatening to other democratic states). [106]

---

[104] Chalmers, Greene & Zhiqiong, op cit:31
[105] Chalmers, Greene & Zhiqiong, op cit:129
[106] Chalmers, Greene & Zhiqiong, op cit:130

Also the emergence of the ASEAN's regional forum (ARF) has been one of the most important attempt to develop region-wide dialogue on security. Although few concrete proposals have emerged, participants, including China, have agreed to exchange information on their defence policies. The ARF has the potential to develop mechanisms to prevent current military build-ups degenerating into a destabilising regional arms race, and seek agreements that Members would not use military force to settle existing disputes.[107]

Conclusion

The rapid economic growth of East Asian countries has contributed to the massive arms build-up in the region. The very high income has led these countries to purchase the 'state-of-the art' sophisticated arms, this has resulted in altering the security of each country in the region. The economic boom and technological progress in East Asia has made the area a market for the most advanced military systems. The countries in this region are changing their present land-oriented armed forces into modern military institutions composing of well-equipped air and naval units which would enable them to deploy military force at sea as well as to far away places, thereby providing them with a capacity for 'power projection'.[108]
2.

Despite the rapid advances in economic growth, the nations in this region face many obstacles over disputed territories which could hinder their cooperation in regional economic and security matters, these disputes remain sources of tension, suspicion, and misunderstandings. All in all the East Asian region faces many challenges such as the possibility of a near-conflict with a potentially nuclear-armed North Korea; war-like talk between China and renegade Taiwan; The spread of airborne platforms, not merely missiles, capable of delivering WMD to targets throughout the East Asian theater is of particular concern to the countries in the region (e.g. North Korea's Hwasong, Rodong and Taepo-Dong 2 ballistic missiles, also the testing of China's M-9, M11 and DF21 nuclear capable ballistic missiles).[109]

Furthermore there is concern of Japanese nuclear capability due to its increase in plutonium reprocessing capability; There is also concern over the proliferation of sophisticated weapons with the capability to strike at long distances, thus giving true power projection capability; In addition, territorial, ethnic, religious and regional disputes still exist within and between some East Asian nations.[110]

There is also concern over China's military posture and development, which have a great impact on the expectations and behaviour of other states in the region. Greater assertiveness in the South China Sea (Spratly Islands) for example, has raised concerns around the region. Although China's leaders explain that their military build-up is defensive and commensurate with China's overall economic growth, others in the region cannot be certain of China's intentions. [111]

Thus, in East Asia, Individual countries therefore find small difficulty in arguing the need to enhance their defence capabilities. Specific objectives include force modernisation, deterrence, power projection, adaptation in some countries to a shift from counter-insurgency priorities to conventional military roles, safeguarding of EEZs through maritime and air patrols, and acquisition of electronic warfare capabilities. Given the rising tensions in the region, this arms build-up could be a catalyst for low-intensity armed conflicts or worse.[112]

Nonetheless, rapid economic growth could reduce the risks of a conflict in East Asia if it is taken in conjunction with confidence building measures. Most of the countries in the area have recognized economic prosperity as their major concern, the region is at this time more at peace than it has been at any time in this century. Therefore numerous governments are seeking to avoid international conflicts in order to focus on their economic growth. The countries in

---

[107] Chalmers, op cit:147
[108] Chalmers, Greene & Zhiqiong, op cit:25
[109] Chalmers, Greene & Zhiqiong, op cit:27
[110] Chalmers, Greene & Zhiqiong, op cit:28
[111] Chalmers, Greene & Zhiqiong, op cit:29
[112] Chalmers, Greene & Zhiqiong, op cit:25

the region are in a process of increased economic and security cooperation, the establishment of APEC (Asia Pacific Economic Cooperation) and the ASEAN Regional Forum (a regional security forum) has further contributed to the economic and social cooperation between the nations. [113]

All in all economic cooperation can provide the basis of regional peace and stability. Many disputes may be solved through fruitful economic co-operation. Furthermore, it is a common experience of the more successful Asian economies that rapid economic growth pulls together diverse groups and regions by providing a sense of shared gain. In contrast, countries which have failed to grow disintegrate, as different groups scramble desperately for their share of a shrinking pie (for instance due to the recent turmoil of the East Asian financial markets there has been much internal conflict, such as between ethnic Chinese and Indonesians which has resulted in many lootings occurring and has resulted in many killings taking place).[114]

The rapid economic growth in East Asia is not sufficient to preserve regional peace and security. Although it has a reasonably good chance of reducing the risks of war it alone cannot prevent conflict in the region, unless other factors such as confidence building measures are taken in conjunction with the rapid advance in economic growth. However, the absence of any serious immediate threat to the region provides the countries in this part of the world to continue prosperous economic development and to start finding possible ways for political change, which will strengthen stability in the region.

Image/pixabay.com/M109 Paladin Howitzer Artillery

---

[113] Chalmers, op cit:221
[114] Cindy Shiner, International Herald Tribune, 1998, p1

Bibliography

Cindy Shiner, International Herald Tribune, 1998

Chapter six: Asia. (2017). *The Military Balance, 117*(1), 237-350.

Bates Gill and J.N Mak, Arms, Transparency and Security in South-East Asia, SIPRI, Oxford University Press, 1997

Ben Dolven, Mark Manyin, Shirley Kan, Maritime Territorial Disputes in East Asia: Issues for Congress, CRS Report, 2014

Chris Taylor, Military Balance in Southeast Asia, House of Commons Library, 2011

IISS, Strategic Survey 2011 – The Annual Review of World Affairs, Routledge, 2011

IISS, Strategic Survey 2012 – The Annual Review of World Affairs, Routledge, 2012

IISS, Strategic Survey 2013 – The Annual Review of World Affairs, Routledge, 2013

J.Goldstein & J. Pevehouse, International Relations, United States, 2007

Malcolm Chalmers, Owen Greene and Xie Zhiqiong, Asia Pacific Security & The UN, University of Bradford, 1995

Malcolm Chalmers, Confidence-Building in South-East Asia, Westview Press, 1996

Mark J. Valencia, Trouble Waters, The Bulletin of the Atomic Scientists, 1997

Michael Beckley, The Emerging Military Balance in East Asia: How China's Neighbours Can Check Chinese Naval Expansion, The MIT Press, 2017

Michael Brown (ed), East Asian Security, The MIT Press, 1996

Michael Klare, East Asia's Militaries Muscle Up, The Bulletin of the Atomic Scientists Publishers, 1997

Nick Bisley, Building Asia's Security, Routledge, 2009

Paul Dibb, Towards a New Balance of Power in Asia, Adelphi Paper 295, Oxford University Press, 1995

Ronald O'Rourke, Maritime Territorial and Exclusive Economic Zone (EEZ) Disputes Involving China: Issues for Congress, CRS Report, 2014

Sean Kay, Global Security in the Twenty-First Century, Rowman & Littlefield Publishers, Inc, 2006

Sidney Bearman, Strategic Survey 1993-1994, Published by Brassey's for the IISS, 1994

The Economist, Asian Security, Published by the Economist Newspaper Ltd, 1996

The Military Balance, 01/2017, Volume 117, Issue 1

Wayne Mapp, Military Modernisation and Buildup in the Asia Pacific – the case for restraint, S.Rajaratnam School of International Studies, 2014

Index

ABOUT THE AUTHOR

Saghir Iqbal is a researcher in International Relations and Security Studies. He is an experienced Intelligence Analyst and has achieved a number of qualifications in this field. He is also a Lecturer in Business Management as well as an Examiner for A Level History and Business. Saghir Iqbal has a subject specialism in the following areas:

International Politics of the Cold War 1945-1991
Conflict Resolution in International Society+
Global and North-South Security Studies
Britain in the World
Disarmament Processes: History and Theory
Nationalism and Ethnicity in Post-Cold War Politics
Middle East: Area in Conflict
European Security
International Politics of the Environment
The United Nations, Peacekeeping and Intervention
Disarmament Processes: Current Problems
Globalisation and the South
International Terrorism
International Politics and Security Studies
Introduction to Peace Studies
Politics of the Global Environment
Regional Security in East Asia
Critical Security studies

www.ingramcontent.com/pod-product-compliance
Lightning Source LLC
Chambersburg PA
CBHW081235250726
48654CB00012B/1333